COLD HEART 'S

BY LUCAS MILLER

THE END

Chapter 1: The Winter Festival's Architect

The crisp winter air nipped at Dora Harrington's cheeks as she stepped out of her car and surveyed the snow-covered village below. Snowflakes, delicate and slow, drifted down, coating the already white landscape in a fine layer of ice. The winding roads of Winterhaven stretched out before her, with its rows of charming cottages tucked beneath heavy blankets of snow, Christmas lights glowing faintly in the early morning fog.

Dora adjusted her scarf, feeling the biting cold slip beneath her tailored coat. This wasn't the kind of job she usually took—designing an entire winter festival in a remote village. But after the last six months of chaos in the city and the toxic breakup she barely managed to crawl out of, Winterhaven felt like a much-needed reprieve. She'd heard about the village's annual winter festival, known for its elaborate snow sculptures and enchanting holiday atmosphere. The festival had a reputation for bringing in tourists, and this year, they had hired her to take it to the next level.

As she reached into the back seat to grab her bag of sketches and notes, the sound of wood chopping echoed in the distance, mingling with the occasional cheer of children playing in the snow. The sense of community here was palpable, and it tugged at something deep inside her, something she thought she had buried long ago.

"Dora?" A voice interrupted her thoughts.

She turned to see Mia, Winterhaven's mayor, striding up to her with a welcoming smile, bundled in a wool coat and a red scarf. The woman had been friendly but persistent in convincing Dora to take on the project. Mia stopped just a few feet away and spread her arms wide.

"Welcome to Winterhaven!" she said, her voice warm despite the cold. "I hope the drive wasn't too rough."

Dora offered a polite smile. "Not at all. It's...quaint."

Mia laughed. "That's the word we go for. Quaint and magical." She glanced around and then motioned for Dora to follow her. "Come on, I'll show you around before the festival team meets you at the community center."

As they walked, Mia gave her the rundown. The festival was scheduled to start in just two weeks, and they had a lot to accomplish before then. Dora had been hired to redesign the layout of the festival grounds, optimize the flow of visitors, and give the snow sculpture garden an aesthetic overhaul.

Dora's eyes flickered over the half-built ice rink, where a handful of people were working to string up lights and secure the perimeter. It looked amateur at best, and she could already see several improvements she'd need to implement. Her mind buzzed with ideas, pulling her back into her professional rhythm.

"Everyone's excited to see what you come up with," Mia said, her voice bright with anticipation. "Especially Oliver."

Dora blinked. "Oliver?"

"Oliver Graham. He's been overseeing the festival for the last few years—sort of our head carpenter and organizer. You'll be working closely with him. He's around here somewhere."

As if summoned by his name, a man appeared from around the corner, carrying a large beam of wood on his shoulder as effortlessly as if it were weightless. Dora's gaze swept over him. Tall, broad-shouldered, with an unruly mop of dark hair that spilled out from under a knit hat, Oliver Graham was every inch the rugged, small-town carpenter she expected him to be. His jacket was speckled with sawdust, and his cheeks were flushed from the cold.

He spotted them, and after setting the beam down near a half-built stall, made his way over. Dora braced herself, knowing this was where things could get tricky. Local organizers often had very different ideas about how things should be done, and despite the mayor's endorsement, she expected resistance.

"Dora, meet Oliver," Mia said cheerfully.

Oliver extended a hand, his eyes assessing her with a hint of curiosity. "You must be the big-city architect."

Dora shook his hand, noting the rough calluses. "That's right."

"I've seen some of your sketches." He nodded to the folder under her arm. "Interesting ideas. A bit ambitious for a place like Winterhaven, don't you think?"

Dora raised an eyebrow. "I've worked on festivals much larger than this. Ambition is what makes them memorable."

Oliver chuckled, a low, throaty sound that caught her off guard. "I'm sure it does. But around here, we like to keep things simple." He turned to Mia. "The town hall needs those light fixtures installed by noon. I'll be back after that."

Dora watched him walk away, feeling her frustration rise. Simplicity was fine, but that didn't mean this festival couldn't be extraordinary. She had ideas that could transform Winterhaven into a true winter wonderland, something far beyond what they had done in previous years. But it was clear Oliver was going to be a challenge.

"He's just being protective," Mia said, sensing the tension. "Oliver's lived here his whole life. He takes pride in keeping the festival true to our traditions."

"I'm not here to change the traditions," Dora said. "Just enhance them."

"I believe you." Mia smiled. "But you'll have to prove it to Oliver. He's not one for fancy designs."

Dora sighed inwardly. It was always the same. People feared change until they saw how much it could benefit them. She'd dealt with tougher clients in the city, and this wasn't any different. At least, that's what she told herself.

As they approached the community center, where the festival team was waiting to meet her, Dora couldn't help but glance back at Oliver. There was something about his easy confidence that rubbed her the wrong way—but also intrigued her. He was grounded in a way that made her feel unsettled, like he saw the world through a lens she couldn't quite understand.

No matter. She was here to do a job. And nothing—not even a stubborn carpenter—was going to get in the way of that.

Chapter 2: Beneath the Surface

Dora was used to busy city streets, the constant hum of traffic, and the blur of faces that passed her by. But here, in Winterhaven, the quiet was unnerving. After her meeting at the community center, she wandered through the village square, her boots crunching in the snow as the soft glow of Christmas lights flickered to life around her.

The square was quaint, like something out of a storybook. A towering Christmas tree dominated the center, its branches weighed down with shimmering ornaments and twinkling lights. Children skated on the half-finished ice rink while their parents chatted and sipped hot cocoa from nearby stalls. In the distance, she could see the outlines of snow sculptures slowly taking form—her own designs still floating in her head, waiting to be realized.

As she walked, Dora's thoughts kept drifting back to Oliver. The way he had spoken to her earlier—so sure of himself, so dismissive of her ideas—had irked her more than she cared to admit. But there was something else, too. Beneath his quiet arrogance, there was a depth, a connection to this place that she couldn't quite shake off.

She rounded a corner and paused as she spotted him in the distance. Oliver stood near the old wooden church, talking to a group of locals. His hat was pulled low over his brow, and his breath hung in the cold air as he laughed at something one of the men had said. For a moment, Dora felt an unexpected pang of curiosity.

What was his story?

Mia had hinted that he was protective of Winterhaven, that his ties to the village ran deep, but she hadn't elaborated. Maybe that was why he was so resistant to her changes. To him, the festival wasn't just an event; it was a reflection of his home, of everything he held dear. But that still didn't excuse his attitude. She was here to make the festival better, not destroy it.

Before she could dwell on it too much, Mia appeared at her side. "Taking in the sights?"

Dora nodded, her gaze still on Oliver. "Something like that."

Mia followed her line of sight and smiled knowingly. "He's a tough one, isn't he?"

"That's an understatement."

Mia chuckled softly. "Don't take it personally. Oliver's always been that way. He's... protective of what's his."

Dora frowned. "The festival?"

Mia shook her head. "The village. His family has lived here for generations. His grandfather started the winter festival decades ago. That's why it means so much to him. He feels like he has to carry on the tradition, keep things the way they've always been."

Dora's eyes widened in surprise. "His grandfather started it?"

"Yep," Mia said, her tone softening. "Oliver practically grew up building snow sculptures and ice rinks. He's poured his heart into this festival every year since he was old enough to hold a hammer. It's more than just a job for him—it's part of his identity."

Dora's frustration ebbed slightly, replaced by a flicker of understanding. She hadn't known that part of the story, hadn't realized just how personal this was for him. No wonder he had bristled at her designs. To him, she was an outsider, coming in to change something he had an emotional stake in.

Still, that didn't mean she was wrong to want to improve things. Tradition was important, yes, but progress could be good, too. There had to be a way to blend both—his vision and hers. But convincing Oliver of that? That would be the real challenge.

Later that evening, after the day's work was done, Dora found herself back at the guesthouse where she was staying. The cozy inn, run by an elderly couple named the Cartwrights, had become her temporary home for the next few weeks. The fireplace crackled in the small common room, and the smell of pine filled the air as Mrs. Cartwright fussed over a pot of tea.

"You're working with Oliver Graham, aren't you?" Mrs. Cartwright asked, settling into the armchair across from Dora.

Dora nodded, surprised by the question. "You know him well?"

"Oh, everyone knows Oliver," Mrs. Cartwright said with a fond smile. "He's like a son to us. His parents passed when he was young, and his grandparents raised him. He's been the heart of this village ever since."

Dora set her tea down, intrigued. "I didn't realize his family was so involved here."

"His grandfather started the winter festival, you know," Mrs. Cartwright continued, her voice tinged with pride. "It's grown over the years, of course, but at its core, it's always been a Graham family tradition. Oliver's been the one to carry it on since his grandparents passed."

Something shifted inside Dora as she listened to the older woman speak. She had been so focused on her own designs, on proving her worth as a city architect, that she hadn't stopped to consider the emotional weight this festival carried for the people of Winterhaven. For Oliver.

The next morning, Dora found herself walking toward the town square with a renewed sense of determination. She had a job to do, yes, but maybe there was a way to blend her vision with the traditions that meant so much to Oliver and the rest of the village.

She spotted him near the snow sculpture garden, inspecting the work of a few volunteers. His breath curled in the cold air, and his hands were tucked into the pockets of his jacket as he gave quiet instructions. Dora hesitated for a moment, then squared her shoulders and approached him.

"Oliver."

He turned at the sound of her voice, his expression unreadable. "Dora."

She swallowed, suddenly unsure of how to begin. "I've been thinking about the festival," she said, her words measured. "And I understand now why it's so important to you. Why the traditions matter."

Oliver raised an eyebrow, his gaze cautious. "And?"

"And," Dora continued, "I want to find a way to honor those traditions while still making this year's festival something special. I'm not here to take away from what your family built. I just want to add to it."

For a long moment, Oliver didn't say anything. He studied her, his eyes flicking over her face as if trying to gauge her sincerity. Finally, he sighed, his breath misting in the air.

"I appreciate that," he said slowly. "But this festival is more than just decorations and sculptures. It's about the people. It's about the memories we've built here. You can't just slap on some fancy designs and expect it to be the same."

Dora nodded. "I know. That's why I'm asking for your help. You know this place better than I do. If we work together, we can create something that blends both our visions."

Oliver's eyes softened, just for a moment, and then he looked away, his jaw tightening. "We'll see," he muttered. "But don't expect me to just roll over and agree to everything."

A small smile tugged at Dora's lips. "I wouldn't dream of it."

As she walked away, she felt a sense of progress. It wasn't much, but it was a start. And maybe, just maybe, Oliver Graham wasn't the immovable mountain she had thought he was.

Chapter 3: Tradition Meets Innovation

The snow had piled higher overnight, and the entire village seemed to glow under the pale light of a cloud-dappled sky. Dora wrapped her coat tighter as she hurried toward the town hall, where the festival committee was scheduled to meet. She was armed with revised sketches, detailed plans, and a newfound determination to find a balance between her designs and Winterhaven's cherished traditions.

The meeting room was small and functional, with wooden beams across the ceiling and a long table that dominated the center. Around the table sat a mix of older villagers—members of the committee who had been part of the festival since its inception. Dora recognized a few faces from around town, including Mrs. Cartwright, the kindly innkeeper who had been one of the first to welcome her. Oliver stood near the back, arms crossed, his expression guarded as always.

Mia was seated at the head of the table, her smile as bright as ever. "Alright, everyone," she said, clapping her hands together. "Let's get started. We're here to review Dora's new ideas for this year's festival."

Dora took a breath and stepped forward, setting her plans on the table. "Thank you all for coming. I've been working hard to ensure that this year's festival remains true to its roots while also bringing in some new elements to make it truly stand out."

She unrolled the sketches, revealing intricate designs for the snow sculpture garden, a more streamlined layout for the festival booths, and improved lighting and decor that would enhance the atmosphere without overshadowing the charm of the village. She explained how the new layout would help with crowd flow, reduce bottlenecks, and create more space for visitors to enjoy the various attractions.

As she spoke, Dora kept an eye on the committee members. Some of them seemed interested, nodding along as she outlined her ideas. But others, like Mrs. Cartwright, exchanged uncertain glances. And then there was Oliver, standing silently in the back, his expression unreadable.

When she finished, Mia smiled encouragingly.
"Thank you, Dora. These are some great ideas. I
think they could really bring something special
to this year's festival."

But before Dora could respond, Mrs. Cartwright
cleared her throat. "I'm sorry, dear, but I have
some concerns," she said, her voice gentle but
firm. "This festival has been the same for as long
as I can remember. People come here because
they love the tradition. They don't want to see it
change."

Several of the other committee members
murmured in agreement. Dora felt her stomach
tighten. She had expected some resistance, but
hearing it from Mrs. Cartwright—the heart of
the village, in many ways—stung more than she
had anticipated.

"I understand that tradition is important," Dora
said carefully, trying to keep her tone calm. "But
progress doesn't have to mean losing what
makes the festival special. I'm not trying to
change everything, just make it more efficient,
more enjoyable for everyone who comes."

Mrs. Cartwright shook her head. "It's just... all
these lights and changes. It's too much. The

festival is supposed to be simple, just like it's always been."

Dora's heart sank as more committee members voiced their concerns. Some worried that the new designs would overwhelm the village's quaint charm, while others feared that her ideas were too ambitious for the budget and resources they had.

"I appreciate your input," Dora said, trying to keep the frustration out of her voice. "But I believe these changes will help attract more visitors and make the festival more successful in the long run."

A tall, thin man named Harold spoke up. He'd been quiet up until now, but his sharp voice cut through the room. "Visitors don't come here for flashy designs. They come here for the tradition, for the sense of community. If we start turning it into a spectacle, we'll lose what makes Winterhaven special."

Dora opened her mouth to respond, but before she could, Oliver stepped forward.

"She's right," he said, his deep voice commanding the room's attention.

The room fell silent, and all eyes turned to Oliver. Even Dora was surprised—he had been so resistant to her ideas before, and now he was defending her?

"The festival does need to evolve," Oliver continued, his gaze sweeping across the room. "If we want to keep it alive, we have to bring in new people, new ideas. Dora's designs might seem big, but they're exactly what we need to make sure Winterhaven doesn't fade into the background. We can still keep the heart of the festival, but we have to be willing to change."

For a moment, no one spoke. Dora could feel the tension in the air, a battle between nostalgia and the need for progress. She glanced at Oliver, still unsure what had made him shift his stance. His words weren't just about the festival—he was speaking as someone who understood the value of keeping the village relevant without losing its soul.

Finally, Mia broke the silence. "Oliver's right," she said gently. "We all love the traditions here, but we also need to think about the future. Dora's ideas could help us do both—honor the past while making sure we're still here for the future."

Mrs. Cartwright sighed softly, folding her hands in her lap. "I suppose we can try," she said, her tone reluctant. "But if it doesn't feel like our festival anymore, we'll have to go back to the way things were."

Dora nodded, grateful for the small victory. "I promise I'll do everything I can to keep the spirit of the festival intact."

The rest of the committee members muttered their agreement, though some still seemed unsure. As the meeting wrapped up and the members began to leave, Mia gave Dora a reassuring smile.

"You did well," she said. "Change is hard for people, but I think they'll come around once they see the results."

Dora smiled back, though her mind was still racing. She had expected resistance, but Oliver's support had caught her off guard. As the room emptied, she gathered her sketches and prepared to leave, only to find Oliver waiting for her by the door.

"Thanks for that," she said, her voice hesitant. "I didn't think you'd back me up like that."

Oliver shrugged, his expression as unreadable as ever. "I don't agree with everything you're doing, but I know the festival needs to grow if it's going to survive. And I've seen your work— you're good at what you do."

Dora raised an eyebrow. "Is that your way of giving me a compliment?"

"Don't get used to it," he said with a slight smirk. "I'm still not convinced about some of your ideas. But I respect that you're trying to make this work for everyone."

Dora studied him for a moment, feeling the tension between them shift ever so slightly. There was still a wall between them, but for the first time, she felt like they might actually be on the same side.

"I'll take what I can get," she said, offering him a small smile.

Oliver nodded, then turned to leave. But just as he reached the door, he paused and glanced back at her.

"If you need help with any of the construction," he said, "let me know. I've got a few ideas on how to make those designs of yours actually work."

Dora blinked in surprise. It wasn't much, but coming from Oliver, it felt like a major concession.

"I'll keep that in mind," she said, watching as he left the room.

As the door closed behind him, Dora felt a strange mix of relief and anticipation. She had won a small victory with the committee, but there was still a long way to go. And now, with Oliver's grudging support, she had an unexpected ally.

Winterhaven was proving to be more complicated than she had expected. But maybe that was exactly what she needed.

Chapter 4: Foundations and Fault Lines

The next morning, the sun peeked through a thick layer of clouds, casting a pale golden light over Winterhaven. Dora could already hear the sounds of construction as she made her way to the festival grounds. Volunteers and local workers bustled about, erecting booths, preparing the snow sculpture area, and arranging holiday lights. But despite the steady hum of activity, her eyes were drawn to one figure in particular—Oliver.

He was standing by the snow sculpture garden, going over some blueprints with a group of workers. Even from a distance, his presence was commanding, the sort of quiet leadership that demanded respect without saying much. As Dora approached, she found herself strangely nervous. She had never been the type to be thrown off by someone's opinion, but Oliver had a way of getting under her skin.

"Morning," she said as she reached his side, her voice steady despite her nerves.

Oliver glanced up from the plans, his sharp blue eyes meeting hers. "Morning. I was just about to check on the framework for the main pavilion. Your designs are good, but there are a few adjustments we'll need to make on-site. The foundation's a bit off."

Dora nodded, slipping into her professional mode. "Show me what needs fixing. We'll get it sorted."

They walked together toward the pavilion area, the crisp air biting at their faces. The construction was well underway, with wooden beams rising from the snow like the skeleton of a grand structure. It was here that the festival's main events would take place: the opening ceremony, the local performances, and the charity auction that raised funds for the village's upkeep each year.

Oliver gestured toward the base of the framework. "The ground here isn't level. If we don't correct it now, the whole structure could shift once the crowds start coming in. We'll need to reinforce it before moving forward."

Dora crouched down, inspecting the foundation with a critical eye. He was right. The uneven terrain could cause problems later, but it wasn't anything they couldn't fix. She glanced up at him, shielding her eyes from the glare of the snow. "I'll get the workers on it. Shouldn't take too long to reinforce."

Oliver nodded, his expression still serious. "Good. We can't afford delays this late in the game."

They stood in silence for a moment, the sounds of construction filling the space between them. Dora was about to move on to the next task when Oliver spoke again, his voice lower, almost reluctant.

"I didn't mean to come down so hard on you before," he said, not quite meeting her eyes. "You came in with a lot of changes, and I guess I was... protective of what this place means to me."

Dora straightened, surprised by the admission. She had been expecting resistance from him the entire time, not an apology—or at least, the closest thing to one she imagined she'd ever get from Oliver Graham.

"I get it," she said after a beat. "This place is your home, your family's legacy. It's personal. I can see why you'd want to keep it the way it's always been."

He glanced at her, something unreadable flickering in his eyes. "It's more than that. The festival... it's the one thing that's held this village together for as long as I can remember. My grandfather started it to give people hope during the winter months. If it changes too much, I'm afraid we'll lose that sense of community."

Dora felt a twinge of understanding. She had come here with the goal of improving the festival, of putting her mark on it. But for Oliver, it wasn't just an event—it was a lifeline for a community that had relied on it for decades. She hadn't fully grasped that before, but now, standing here with him, she could see it more clearly.

"I don't want to take that away," she said softly. "I want to add to it, make it even better for the future. But I promise, I'll make sure we don't lose what makes it special."

Oliver held her gaze for a moment longer, then gave a small nod. "Alright. Let's see if we can make this work."

For the next few hours, they worked side by side, overseeing the construction and making adjustments as needed. It wasn't the most glamorous part of the job, but it was necessary. And as the day wore on, Dora found herself falling into an easy rhythm with Oliver. He wasn't as cold or dismissive as he had seemed at first. In fact, when they were focused on the task at hand, they worked well together.

At one point, they stood back to watch as the workers raised the first section of the pavilion roof. The beams creaked as they were lifted into place, but everything held steady. Dora let out a breath she hadn't realized she was holding.

"Looks good," Oliver said, crossing his arms over his chest as he surveyed the progress.

"Yeah," Dora agreed, feeling a small sense of accomplishment. "It's coming together."

Oliver glanced at her, a faint smile tugging at the corner of his mouth. "You know, for a city architect, you're not half bad at this."

Dora raised an eyebrow, a teasing smile on her lips. "Is that your way of giving me another compliment?"

"Don't push your luck."

She laughed softly, the tension between them easing for the first time since she had arrived in Winterhaven. It wasn't exactly friendship, but it was something—an understanding, perhaps. They might not see eye to eye on everything, but they were both working toward the same goal.

As the afternoon wore on, Dora found herself growing more comfortable in Oliver's presence. They debated design choices, exchanged ideas, and even shared a few moments of light banter. It was a far cry from their first few tense interactions, and Dora couldn't help but feel a small sense of victory. She was finally breaking through his tough exterior.

But as they finished up for the day and prepared to leave the site, Dora noticed something else. The way Oliver's eyes lingered on the pavilion, the way his shoulders tensed slightly as he looked around at the festival grounds—it wasn't just about the festival. There was something deeper, something personal that he wasn't sharing.

She didn't press him on it, though. Not yet. Instead, she focused on the work ahead, on making sure that the festival would be a success. There would be time to unravel Oliver's secrets later.

As they walked back toward the village square, the cold biting at their cheeks, Oliver turned to her with a hint of a smile. "You up for another round tomorrow? We've got a lot more work to do."

Dora smirked, her breath visible in the frosty air. "I'll be here. Just try to keep up."

Oliver chuckled, shaking his head. "We'll see about that."

They parted ways at the square, and as Dora made her way back to the guesthouse, she couldn't shake the feeling that something had shifted between them. It wasn't just the professional collaboration—it was the way they had started to trust each other, even if only a little.

But as much as she was beginning to understand Oliver, there was still so much she didn't know. And the more time she spent with him, the more she realized that her work in Winterhaven wasn't just about the festival. It was about the people. About Oliver.

And maybe, just maybe, about finding something she hadn't even been looking for.

Chapter 5: Cracks in the Snow

The next morning dawned clear but bitterly cold, the kind of cold that seeped through layers of clothing and bit at any exposed skin. Dora wrapped her scarf tighter around her neck as she made her way back to the festival grounds, her breath visible in the freezing air. Today was crucial. With only a few days left before the festival opened, every detail needed to be perfect. The pavilion was nearly complete, and the sculpture garden was starting to take shape. Everything was on track.

As she arrived at the site, she noticed the workers milling around the pavilion, their voices low and urgent. Oliver stood in the center of the group, his face tense, his arms crossed tightly over his chest.

Dora quickened her pace, a knot forming in her stomach. Something was wrong.

"What's going on?" she asked as she approached, her eyes scanning the pavilion for any visible issues.

Oliver turned to her, his expression grim. "We've got a problem."

He motioned toward the base of the pavilion, where one of the supporting beams had shifted out of place. The structure leaned slightly to one side, the wood creaking ominously in the cold wind. Dora's heart sank as she saw the cracks in the snow-packed ground beneath the pavilion.

"It's the foundation," Oliver said, his voice low but controlled. "The ground underneath must have softened from the temperature fluctuations over the past few days. The supports aren't stable anymore."

Dora knelt down to inspect the damage, her mind racing. The ground had seemed solid enough when they started construction, but with the constant freezing and thawing, it had become a ticking time bomb. If the pavilion wasn't stabilized quickly, it could collapse entirely, and the festival's main attraction would be lost.

"How bad is it?" she asked, standing up and brushing snow off her gloves.

Oliver's jaw tightened. "Bad enough. We need to reinforce the entire foundation, and we're going to have to do it fast. If we don't, we'll have to tear the whole thing down and start over."

The weight of his words settled heavily on Dora's shoulders. The pavilion was one of the centerpiece attractions of the festival. Without it, the event would lose much of its appeal, and they were running out of time to fix the problem. She glanced around at the workers, most of whom were already looking uneasy.

"Can we do it?" she asked, turning back to Oliver.

His eyes narrowed as he calculated the logistics in his head. "We can, but it's going to take a lot of manpower, and we'll need to bring in more supplies. The cold's going to make everything harder."

Dora took a deep breath, her mind racing through possible solutions. There was no way they could afford to delay the festival, not with so much already riding on it. They would have to work through the night if necessary, and she would have to rally the town's volunteers to pitch in.

"Alright," she said, her voice steady despite the panic clawing at her chest. "Let's get started.

We'll reinforce the supports with additional beams and pack the ground with gravel to stabilize the foundation. I'll handle the volunteers and get more supplies."

Oliver nodded, already moving toward the workers to give them instructions. Dora watched him for a moment, marveling at how quickly he switched into problem-solving mode. She felt a small spark of admiration for his calm under pressure, but there was no time to dwell on it. They had work to do.

Dora hurried back toward the town square, where Mia and a few other festival organizers were setting up decorations. She explained the situation as quickly as she could, her voice betraying none of the anxiety she felt.

"We need more people at the construction site," Dora said, her breath coming out in visible puffs. "The pavilion's foundation is compromised, and we're running out of time to fix it."

Mia's eyes widened in alarm, but she didn't hesitate. "I'll gather whoever's available. We'll send as many volunteers as we can."

Within the hour, a small army of volunteers had gathered at the festival grounds. The air buzzed with tension as Dora and Oliver directed the workers, assigning them tasks and explaining how to reinforce the structure. It was a daunting task, especially with the freezing temperatures, but everyone seemed determined to save the pavilion.

As the day wore on, Dora found herself working side by side with Oliver, digging into the snow and frozen earth, measuring out support beams, and ensuring that each new piece of the foundation was secure. The cold seeped into her bones, her muscles aching from the strain, but she pushed through, refusing to let the setback defeat her.

At one point, as they were hammering a beam into place, Oliver glanced over at her, his breath visible in the frigid air. "You're tougher than you look."

Dora grinned, though her arms were trembling from the effort. "Don't let the city background fool you. I can handle myself."

Oliver chuckled, but his eyes remained serious. "We'll get this done, but we're cutting it close."

She nodded, wiping sweat from her brow despite the cold. "We have to. This festival is too important."

As the afternoon wore on, the pace of work increased. More volunteers arrived, carrying supplies and offering whatever help they could. It was a frantic effort, but there was a certain energy in the air—a shared sense of purpose that kept everyone pushing forward.

By the time the sun began to set, the pavilion was finally starting to look stable again. Dora's legs felt like jelly, and her hands were numb from the cold, but the sight of the reinforced structure filled her with a sense of accomplishment.

Oliver stood beside her, his breath heavy from the exertion. "We'll need to check it again in the morning to make sure everything's holding, but I think we've got it under control."

Dora nodded, too exhausted to speak. She looked around at the volunteers, most of whom were starting to pack up and head home for the night. The work wasn't done yet, but they had made significant progress. The festival could still happen.

As the last of the workers left, Dora and Oliver lingered for a moment longer, standing in the quiet of the snow-covered grounds. The village lights twinkled in the distance, casting a soft glow over the scene.

"You did good today," Oliver said quietly, his voice cutting through the stillness.

Dora glanced at him, surprised by the compliment. "I couldn't have done it without everyone's help."

He nodded, his expression thoughtful. "Still. You're the one who kept it all together."

Dora smiled faintly, feeling the weight of the day lift just a little. "I wasn't sure if we were going to pull it off."

Oliver's gaze softened, and for the first time, there was no tension between them, no lingering resentment or guardedness. Just two people, standing in the cold, sharing a quiet moment of victory.

"We'll make it through," he said, his voice low and certain.

Dora looked at him, feeling a strange warmth in the pit of her stomach despite the cold. She didn't know what was happening between them—whether it was just the relief of a crisis averted or something more—but for the first time since she'd arrived in Winterhaven, she felt like she belonged.

"Yeah," she murmured. "We will."

Chapter 6: Fractures in the Plan

The next morning, the village was blanketed in a fresh layer of snow. The crisp air and calm skies made everything seem peaceful, a sharp contrast to the chaos of the previous day. Dora felt a flicker of relief as she arrived at the festival grounds and saw the pavilion still standing strong. The reinforcements had held, and it looked as though the structure would survive.

Oliver was already there, inspecting the beams and supports. When he saw her, he gave a quick nod of acknowledgment. The lingering tension from their earlier clashes had evaporated after their late-night collaboration, replaced with a cautious camaraderie.

"Everything looks good," Oliver said, his breath clouding in the cold air. "We'll have to keep an eye on it, but I think we're in the clear."

Dora smiled, the weight of the previous day's anxiety easing. "I'll take that as a win."

But just as she was beginning to relax, her phone buzzed in her pocket. Dora pulled it out and glanced at the screen, expecting an update from one of the festival organizers. Instead, her heart sank as she read the message.

We regret to inform you that due to unforeseen budget constraints, Winter's Embrace will no longer be able to sponsor the Winterhaven Festival. We wish you the best of luck in your endeavors.

Dora stared at the message, her pulse quickening. Winter's Embrace was the festival's largest sponsor—a luxury winter apparel company that had pledged a significant amount of money to support the event. Without their contribution, the festival's budget would be severely compromised.

Her fingers hovered over the screen, unsure of how to respond. What could she even say? The festival was days away, and now they were facing a financial crisis that could cripple everything they'd worked for.

Oliver noticed her hesitation. "Something wrong?"

Dora hesitated, then handed him the phone, letting him read the message for himself. His face darkened as he scanned the text.

"Damn," he muttered, running a hand through his hair. "That's a huge blow."

Dora nodded, her mind racing. "We can't afford to lose them. They were covering almost half the budget for the event. Without that money, we won't be able to pay for the final decorations, the performers, or even the equipment rentals."

Oliver's jaw tightened. "Is there any chance we can convince them to reconsider?"

Dora shook her head, frustration bubbling to the surface. "I doubt it. If they've already made this decision, it's probably final."

Oliver cursed under his breath, pacing in the snow. "We're too close to the festival to find another sponsor of that size."

Dora felt the weight of the situation pressing down on her. They had been so focused on the logistics and construction that she hadn't anticipated a financial disaster like this. Everything was hanging by a thread, and now that thread was about to snap.

"I'll make some calls," she said, trying to sound more confident than she felt. "Maybe there's a local business that can step in, or we can crowdfund some of the remaining costs. It's a long shot, but it's better than doing nothing."

Oliver nodded, his frustration giving way to determination. "We'll figure something out. I can talk to the council—see if they can allocate some emergency funds. They won't be happy about it, but we can't let the festival fall apart."

Dora appreciated his willingness to help, but she knew that even with the council's support, they'd still be far short of the funds needed to pull off the festival as planned. She would have to think fast and come up with a creative solution—something that would rally the town's support and make up for the financial shortfall.

As she began making calls to local businesses, Dora couldn't shake the sense of dread creeping up her spine. Every rejection felt like another blow to the festival's chances. Most businesses were already stretched thin for the winter season and couldn't afford to contribute more.

Hours passed, and Dora was no closer to securing the funds they needed. She leaned against the side of the pavilion, her fingers numb from the cold, her phone heavy in her hand. The village square around her bustled with preparations, unaware of the looming crisis.

Just as she was about to give up for the day, her phone buzzed again. This time, it was Mia.

"Hey, I've got some news," Mia said, her voice unusually upbeat. "It's not exactly a new sponsor, but I might have found something that could help us out."

Dora straightened, her heart pounding with a flicker of hope. "What is it?"

"There's a local philanthropist, someone who's been looking for a big project to support. Apparently, they've been interested in helping the village for a while, but they didn't want to get involved unless it was something major."

Dora's pulse quickened. "Do you think they'd be willing to step in and help fund the festival?"

"I think it's possible. They're a bit of a recluse, though. I've only heard whispers about them, but from what I understand, they've got deep pockets and a soft spot for Winterhaven."

Dora's mind raced. This was their chance, but they needed to act fast. "Do you have any way of contacting them?"

Mia paused. "Not directly, but I know someone who might be able to arrange a meeting. It's a long shot, but it's better than nothing."

Dora didn't hesitate. "Let's set it up. We don't have time to waste."

Later that afternoon, Dora found herself sitting in a cozy but dimly lit room, the crackle of a fire the only sound as she waited for Winterhaven's mysterious benefactor to arrive. She had barely had time to catch her breath before Mia had whisked her away to this secluded cabin on the outskirts of town.

The door creaked open, and a tall, slender woman with silver-streaked hair stepped inside. She moved with an air of quiet authority, her dark eyes sharp and calculating as they swept over Dora.

"I understand you're in a bit of trouble," the woman said, her voice smooth but with an edge that suggested she was not one to waste time on pleasantries.

Dora stood, offering a polite smile despite her nerves. "Yes. We've lost our primary sponsor for the festival, and without their funding, we might not be able to go through with it. We're hoping you might be willing to help."

The woman, whose name Dora had learned was Evelyn Reed, studied her for a long moment, as though weighing her response. Finally, she spoke.

"I've lived in this village for a long time, Miss Hart. Longer than most people realize. I've watched it grow and change, and I've always believed in its potential. But what I don't believe in is throwing money at a cause that isn't worth the investment."

Dora's stomach tightened. She hadn't expected this to be easy, but Evelyn's cold, business-like demeanor was making it even more difficult than she had anticipated.

"We're not just asking for money," Dora said, her voice steady. "We're asking for a chance to keep this community alive. The festival is more than just an event—it's a way to bring people together, to support local businesses, and to give the village something to look forward to during the darkest months of the year."

Evelyn raised an eyebrow, clearly unimpressed. "And why should I believe that you can pull it off, especially now that you've lost your primary backer?"

Dora hesitated for a fraction of a second, but then she spoke with conviction. "Because we've already come this far. We've faced setback after setback, but we've kept going. We're not going to let a financial hurdle stop us, and with your help, we can make sure the festival is everything this village needs it to be."

For a moment, Evelyn said nothing. Then, slowly, she nodded. "I'll consider it. But I'll want to see a full breakdown of your plans and how you intend to make up for the shortfall. If I'm going to invest, I want to know it's a sound decision."

Dora exhaled, relieved that she hadn't been dismissed outright. "Of course. I'll have the details ready for you by tomorrow."

Evelyn smiled faintly, though it didn't quite reach her eyes. "Good. I look forward to seeing what you come up with."

As Evelyn left the room, Dora felt a mixture of relief and apprehension. They weren't out of the woods yet, but this was the closest they'd come to a solution.

Now, it was up to her to make sure the proposal was airtight—and to convince Evelyn Reed that Winterhaven was worth saving.

Chapter 7: A Heartfelt Appeal

The following morning, Dora arrived at the town hall earlier than usual, her nerves running high. She held a folder filled with meticulously prepared notes, budget breakdowns, and a detailed timeline of festival events. She'd worked through the night, determined to create a proposal that would win over Evelyn Reed. But she knew facts and figures alone wouldn't be enough.

Oliver joined her in the meeting room, looking just as tired but equally focused. He gave her a nod, a silent gesture of solidarity. Despite their initial clashes, they had become a team, bound by their shared commitment to making the Winterhaven Festival a success.

Evelyn arrived precisely on time. Her sharp gaze swept over both of them as she took a seat at the head of the table. Dora couldn't help but feel a ripple of anxiety as Evelyn's cool, calculating demeanor settled over the room.

"Let's get straight to it," Evelyn said, her voice cutting through the silence. "You've prepared your proposal, I assume."

Dora took a deep breath and handed her the folder. "Yes, everything is outlined here. We've detailed the costs, the expected revenues, and how we plan to manage the event."

Evelyn flipped through the documents without much expression. For several minutes, the room was filled only with the sound of pages turning and the crackle of the fire in the corner. Dora glanced at Oliver, who sat rigid in his chair, his fingers laced tightly together.

Finally, Evelyn closed the folder and looked up. "It's thorough. I'll give you that. But numbers aren't the problem. My concern is whether or not this festival is worth the investment."

Dora straightened in her seat, prepared to launch into her defense, but before she could speak, Oliver leaned forward, his tone unexpectedly calm.

"This festival isn't just about numbers, Ms. Reed," Oliver said. "It's about the people here. It's about giving this community something to rally around."

Evelyn's brow furrowed, but she didn't interrupt, and Dora watched, intrigued, as Oliver continued.

"I've been part of this village for years," he said. "I've seen it go through hard times—people moving away, businesses closing down, and fewer and fewer reasons for anyone to stay. This festival isn't just a tradition; it's a reminder of why Winterhaven matters. Why it's worth staying."

Evelyn leaned back in her chair, her fingers resting on the folder. "And what makes you think I care about the people in this village?"

Dora's heart skipped a beat at the question, but Oliver didn't flinch. Instead, he smiled, the faintest trace of warmth breaking through his usual stoicism.

"I don't think you're here because you want to save us," Oliver said. "I think you're here because you already care, even if you don't want to admit it."

The room went quiet. Evelyn's expression didn't change immediately, but there was a subtle shift in her posture—a tension releasing, as if Oliver's words had struck a chord.

Dora decided to step in, her voice soft but resolute. "Ms. Reed, we know you've lived here for a long time. You've seen this village change, and you've watched it go through highs and lows. But there's something special about Winterhaven, something worth fighting for. This festival is more than just an event; it's a way to remind people of that."

Evelyn's gaze flicked between them, but this time, there was no sharpness in her eyes. She seemed to be weighing their words carefully, as though she, too, was struggling with something deeper than a business decision.

For a moment, it seemed as if Evelyn would stand up and walk away. But then, much to their surprise, she spoke in a quiet, almost reflective tone.

"You're right," she said softly. "I've seen this village go through more than most people here realize. I've watched it thrive and falter, and through it all, I've stayed. But Winterhaven isn't what it used to be. I don't see the same spirit I once did."

Dora exchanged a glance with Oliver, sensing they were getting closer to the heart of the matter.

"That's why the festival is so important," Dora said, her voice steady. "It's a chance to rekindle that spirit, to remind people what this village can be when we come together."

Evelyn's eyes narrowed slightly, but there was a glimmer of something other than skepticism—a flicker of emotion that hadn't been there before.

"When I was younger," Evelyn began, her voice distant, "Winterhaven was known for its festivals. People from neighboring towns would come to see what we had to offer—our crafts, our food, our hospitality. It was a place people wanted to be. But over time, that faded. Businesses closed, people moved away, and the festivals became smaller, more forgettable."

She paused, her gaze drifting to the window, where snowflakes were gently falling.

"I stayed because this village was my home. But now... I wonder if it's worth saving."

Dora's throat tightened at the sadness in Evelyn's voice. For the first time, she saw Evelyn not as a cold, business-minded benefactor but as someone who had a deep, personal connection to the village—a connection she had been hiding beneath her sharp exterior.

"It is worth saving," Dora said, her voice barely above a whisper. "We've come together before, and we can do it again. This festival is our chance to remind everyone why Winterhaven is special."

Evelyn didn't respond immediately. Instead, she sat in silence, her gaze still fixed on the snow outside. For several long moments, Dora and Oliver waited, unsure of what would happen next.

Finally, Evelyn turned back to them, her expression unreadable. "I'll fund the festival," she said, her voice firm but quiet. "But only if you're willing to make it something worth remembering. I don't want a mediocre event with half-hearted decorations and lackluster performances. If we're going to do this, we do it right."

Dora felt a surge of relief and excitement, though she tried to keep her emotions in check. "We'll make it the best festival Winterhaven has seen in years," she promised. "You won't regret it."

Evelyn's lips curved into a faint smile—perhaps the first real smile Dora had seen from her. "I'm holding you to that."

Later that day, as Dora and Oliver walked back through the village square, their footsteps crunching in the fresh snow, a sense of cautious optimism filled the air between them.

"We did it," Dora said, the realization slowly sinking in.

Oliver chuckled. "You did it. You were the one who convinced her."

Dora shook her head. "No, we both did. She needed to hear from both of us—about the community, about why this festival matters."

Oliver nodded, glancing at her with a rare look of approval. "I guess we make a pretty good team after all."

Dora smiled, the tension that had hung between them for days finally beginning to ease. The weight of the festival's success still pressed on her shoulders, but for the first time in days, she felt like they had a real chance to pull it off.

As they passed by the pavilion, now glistening under the soft glow of the streetlights, Dora couldn't help but feel a renewed sense of hope. Winterhaven's festival was back on track, and with Evelyn's support, they could make it something truly unforgettable.

But beneath that hope, a flicker of uncertainty remained. They had overcome this hurdle, but the real work was just beginning.

Chapter 8: A Growing Bond

The next few weeks flew by in a whirlwind of activity. With Evelyn's unexpected support, Dora and Oliver were determined to make the Winterhaven Festival a resounding success. They held meetings almost every day, brainstorming ideas, organizing tasks, and liaising with vendors and performers. Each day felt like a marathon, but there was an electric energy in the air that fueled them.

Dora had always thought of Oliver as a colleague, someone she had to work with to achieve a common goal. But now, as they spent countless hours together, her perspective began to shift. She found herself stealing glances at him, captivated by the way he furrowed his brow in concentration or the way a small smile tugged at his lips when he was genuinely pleased with a suggestion.

One afternoon, they found themselves alone in the town hall's conference room, poring over final details for the festival's opening night. The sun streamed through the tall windows, casting a warm glow across the room. Dora leaned over the table, her fingers dancing across the spreadsheets filled with costs and schedules.

"Okay, so we have the ice sculptor confirmed, and the music lineup is finalized," Oliver said, a hint of excitement in his voice. He looked up from the documents and met her gaze, his dark eyes sparkling with enthusiasm. "I think this is really coming together."

"It is," Dora replied, her heart racing as she smiled back at him. "I can't believe how far we've come in such a short time. I was so worried about convincing Evelyn, but now... it feels like we have a real chance to create something amazing."

Oliver nodded, his expression shifting to one of sincerity. "You did more than just convince her. You brought this whole thing back to life. I'm not sure I would've had the confidence to go against her if you hadn't pushed me."

Dora felt a flush of warmth at his words. "I couldn't have done it without you. Your insights and experience have been invaluable. It's like we complement each other."

He chuckled softly, the sound sending a pleasant shiver down her spine. "I guess we make a pretty good team after all, huh?"

Just then, the door swung open, and Evelyn stepped in, her usual brisk demeanor softened by a hint of approval. "I hope I'm not interrupting," she said, glancing at the papers scattered across the table. "I wanted to see how everything was progressing."

Dora and Oliver quickly sat up straighter, shifting into a more professional stance. "Everything's on track," Dora replied, her voice steady. "We've confirmed the vendors and the schedule is coming together nicely."

Evelyn nodded, her lips curving into a satisfied smile. "Good. I'm impressed with your work so far. Just remember, quality is key. I want this festival to shine, and that means no corners cut."

"Absolutely," Oliver said. "We're committed to making it the best we can."

As Evelyn continued to discuss logistics, Dora stole another glance at Oliver. He was engaged, leaning slightly forward, his intensity evident as he listened to Evelyn. There was something undeniably magnetic about him, something that drew her in.

As the meeting wrapped up, Evelyn left them with a few final instructions and stepped out, leaving Dora and Oliver alone once again. A silence settled over the room, charged with an unspoken tension that hung thick in the air.

"Did you notice how she seemed more relaxed today?" Dora asked, trying to break the tension. "Maybe she's finally starting to see the potential in this festival."

Oliver nodded, his eyes still focused on the door. "It seems that way. I think she wants this to work, too, even if she won't admit it."

Dora chuckled softly, the sound echoing slightly in the empty room. "Maybe we should throw in a surprise performance from her favorite band. That would win her over."

Oliver grinned, a playful glint in his eyes. "That might just do the trick. But what do you think we should do about the fire juggling act? We need to keep things exciting!"

Dora laughed, feeling a rush of warmth that pushed aside the stress of their work. "I think juggling fire will definitely keep the audience on their toes!"

In that moment, the banter flowed effortlessly between them, and Dora found herself leaning closer, drawn to the connection that was blossoming. With every shared joke, every lingering glance, she felt something shift between them. It was exhilarating and terrifying all at once.

But as they wrapped up their work for the day, a sense of uncertainty washed over Dora. Was it the excitement of the festival, or was it something more personal that was causing her heart to race whenever she was near Oliver? She couldn't quite tell anymore.

"Hey, do you want to grab a coffee before heading home?" Oliver asked, breaking through her thoughts.

Dora hesitated, her heart fluttering at the suggestion. "Sure, that sounds nice."

They walked to a small café just down the street, the air crisp and fragrant with the scent of brewing coffee. As they settled into a cozy corner, Dora watched Oliver as he stirred his drink, the light catching the contours of his face, illuminating the intensity of his focus.

"What about you?" she asked, leaning in slightly. "What do you want from this festival?"

Oliver paused, looking up at her with a thoughtful expression. "Honestly? I want to see the village come alive again. It's been too quiet for too long, and I want to be part of something that brings people together."

Dora felt a wave of admiration wash over her. "I get that. It's easy to lose sight of what really matters in a small town like this. But I think this festival could be a turning point for us."

He nodded, a spark of determination igniting in his eyes. "Yeah, I believe that, too. We can do this."

As they talked about their hopes for the festival and the community, a sense of camaraderie deepened between them. They shared stories of their childhoods, laughter spilling over as they recounted their most embarrassing moments. With each passing minute, the bond they were building felt more significant.

But as the conversation shifted, Dora could sense the mood changing. There was an intensity in Oliver's gaze that made her heart race again, and she couldn't help but wonder if he felt it too.

"Dora," he said, his voice low and earnest, "I want you to know… I appreciate everything you've done. You've put your heart into this project, and it shows."

Her breath caught in her throat as she met his gaze, vulnerability reflected in his dark eyes. "Thank you, Oliver. That means a lot."

He reached across the table, his hand brushing against hers, sending a spark of electricity between them. "I don't want this to just be about the festival. I want to know you better, too."

Dora's pulse quickened, and she could feel the heat rising in her cheeks. "I'd like that."

But just as the moment hung in the air, a loud burst of laughter interrupted them, pulling their attention to a group of friends who had entered the café. The spell was broken, and Oliver pulled his hand back, the moment dissipating like a dream.

As they finished their coffees, Dora couldn't shake the feeling of longing that had settled in her chest. She could sense a shift in her feelings for Oliver, a deeper connection forming, but the timing felt precarious with the festival looming ahead.

Chapter 9: Festival Preparations Intensify

As the festival date drew closer, excitement buzzed through Winterhaven like static electricity. The town was abuzz with preparations, and Dora and Oliver were in the thick of it. The duo spent late nights organizing schedules, coordinating with vendors, and ensuring every detail was accounted for. Yet, amid the flurry of activity, tensions began to simmer beneath the surface.

One brisk morning, as Dora entered the town hall, she found Oliver already poring over the latest logistics report. He looked up, a frown etching his brow.

"Hey, you're early," he said, pushing a stray hair from his face. "I was just looking at the numbers from the vendor contracts. We're over budget by a bit."

Dora's stomach sank. "Over budget? How much?"

"About fifteen percent," he replied, crossing his arms as he leaned back In his chair. "If we don't adjust somewhere, it's going to be a problem."

Dora sighed, running a hand through her hair. "We can't compromise on quality. Not now. The festival needs to make an impact if we want to bring people back next year."

"I agree," Oliver replied, but there was an edge to his voice. "But we need to be realistic. We can't pull off this event if we're bleeding money."

Dora felt frustration rising. "So, what do you propose? Cutting the fire juggling act? Skimping on the decorations? We've worked too hard for this!"

He met her gaze, his expression firm but understanding. "I'm not suggesting we cut corners, but we need to find a balance. We can't risk going into the red over this. I think we should consider scaling back a few things—maybe the lighting or the smaller performances."

Dora opened her mouth to argue, but she could see the logic in his suggestion. Still, the thought of cutting back on their plans felt like a betrayal of everything they had worked for. "Scaling back isn't an option. We need to go all out for this festival."

"Dora," Oliver said, his tone calming. "I'm on your side. I want this to be a success just as much as you do. But if we don't come to a compromise, we could end up in serious trouble. I just want to make sure we're being smart about this."

The intensity of their conversation hung heavy in the air, and Dora felt the weight of her emotions. She wanted to argue, but she also respected Oliver's perspective. The thought of letting him down gnawed at her.

"Okay," she finally said, her voice softening. "Let's look at the numbers together. Maybe there's a middle ground we can find."

Oliver's expression shifted, relief washing over his features. "Thank you. I know this is tough, but we can figure it out."

As they dug into the reports, the tension slowly began to dissipate. They worked side by side, crunching numbers and discussing which elements could be adjusted without sacrificing quality. Dora appreciated Oliver's insights, and it was refreshing to collaborate rather than butt heads.

A couple of hours later, they had reached a compromise. They would cut a few smaller acts and trim some of the extravagant decorations, but the core of the festival—the ice sculptures, the music lineup, and the main performances— would remain intact.

"See? That wasn't so hard," Oliver said, a teasing smile breaking across his face.

Dora rolled her eyes but couldn't help but grin. "You're not going to let me forget that, are you?"

"Not a chance," he replied, laughter dancing in his eyes.

Just then, Evelyn walked in, her presence commanding as she looked between them. "I trust you two have everything under control?"

"Yes," Dora said, trying to sound more confident than she felt. "We worked out a plan to stay within budget without sacrificing quality."

Evelyn raised an eyebrow, her lips pressing together in a thin line. "That's good to hear. We can't afford to cut corners, but we also can't afford to lose sight of the bigger picture. Make sure everyone is on the same page."

Dora nodded, feeling a renewed sense of determination. "Absolutely. We'll keep everyone informed."

As Evelyn moved on to check on other aspects of the festival, Oliver turned back to Dora, his expression serious. "I know it was tough, but I'm glad we managed to find a solution together. You really care about this festival, don't you?"

"I do," she replied, a hint of vulnerability in her voice. "This festival means everything to me. It's about more than just bringing people together; it's about reminding us of what we can achieve when we work as a community."

He studied her for a moment, a softness in his gaze. "I can see that. You're passionate about it. It's inspiring."

Dora felt her heart race, the sincerity in his words sending a thrill through her. "Thanks, Oliver. That means a lot."

As they continued to work through the day, the atmosphere gradually shifted from tension to camaraderie. They tackled each problem together, brainstorming ideas, and finding solutions in unison. The warmth between them grew stronger, each shared laugh and lingering glance weaving a thread of connection that was hard to ignore.

But just as the day began to wind down, disaster struck. Dora received a frantic call from one of the main vendors, their voice a mixture of panic and disbelief.

"Dora, I'm so sorry. We've had a last-minute emergency. We can't provide the fireworks display for the opening night."

Dora felt her heart drop. "What? No fireworks? That's a centerpiece of the festival!"

"I know, and I'm really sorry! We tried to find a replacement, but there's nothing available on such short notice. We'll do our best to work with you next year, but I don't know what else to say!"

Dora hung up, her mind racing. She turned to Oliver, who had been quietly observing her conversation. "The fireworks vendor pulled out," she said, her voice shaky. "We need to find a replacement, or the opening night is going to fall flat."

"What do you mean? Is there time to get someone else?" Oliver asked, his eyes narrowing in concern.

Dora shook her head, her heart pounding. "It's too late for someone to secure permits, and most vendors are already booked for the season. If we can't find an alternative, we might have to rethink the whole opening night."

Oliver took a deep breath, his expression resolute. "We can't let that happen. Let's brainstorm. Maybe we can find a creative solution that won't rely on traditional fireworks."

As they began to brainstorm, an idea sparked in Dora's mind. "What if we used a light show instead? It could be something really unique and beautiful, and it could tie into the theme of winter and the magic of the season."

Oliver's eyes lit up. "That could work! We'd just need to find a company that specializes in light displays."

Dora nodded, a flicker of hope igniting in her chest. "I'll start making calls. If we act fast, we might still pull this off."

But as she dialed number after number, her heart sank with each rejection. Most companies were either unavailable or had already booked for the festival weekend. The weight of failure pressed heavily on her, and she could feel her hopes dwindling.

"Dora, don't get discouraged," Oliver said, his voice steady. "We'll find someone. We have to."

Hours passed, and Dora's frustration mounted. She hated feeling powerless and knew that if they didn't secure something soon, the festival's opening night would be a disaster.

Just when she thought all hope was lost, her phone buzzed. It was a small company from a nearby town that specialized in synchronized light displays. They had just finished a job and could fit them in for the festival if they could secure the permits in time.

"I think I found someone!" Dora exclaimed, her voice breaking with excitement. "They can do a light show if we can get the permits processed immediately!"

Oliver's face broke into a grin, relief washing over him. "That's amazing! Let's call Evelyn and get her on board with the idea."

As they contacted Evelyn, the adrenaline coursed through Dora's veins. She felt a renewed sense of purpose, buoyed by Oliver's unwavering support. Together, they presented the idea of the light show to Evelyn, who initially hesitated but ultimately agreed.

"This could work," Evelyn said, her eyes gleaming with interest. "But you need to make sure everything goes smoothly. I'll help with the permits, but you two need to oversee the setup and execution."

"Absolutely," Dora replied, determination surging through her. "We won't let you down."

As they worked late into the night finalizing the details, a sense of unity formed between them. The adrenaline of solving the crisis fused with the electric connection they shared, and Dora couldn't shake the feeling that something significant was developing.

Chapter 10: The Night Before the Festival

The sun dipped below the horizon, casting a warm, golden glow over Winterhaven. The townsfolk were bustling about, finalizing their preparations for the festival, and a sense of anticipation hung in the air. As Dora and Oliver stood in the middle of the town square, surrounded by twinkling fairy lights and the aroma of freshly baked goods, an electric excitement surged between them.

"Can you believe it? Tomorrow is the big day," Dora said, glancing around at the transformation of the town. The square was a kaleidoscope of colors, with stalls adorned in bright ribbons and decorations celebrating the winter season.

"I know," Oliver replied, his eyes shining with enthusiasm. "It's incredible to see everything come together. I think it's going to be a night to remember."

Dora's heart raced at his words. It wasn't just the festival that excited her; it was the growing connection she felt with Oliver. He had been her partner in crime through all the chaos, and as they stood there together, she felt a warmth spreading through her chest.

"I couldn't have done it without you," she said, sincerity dripping from her voice. "Your input was invaluable. I was so caught up in my vision that I didn't even consider alternatives. You really saved us."

Oliver turned to her, a soft smile gracing his lips. "You give me too much credit. This was a team effort. Your passion and dedication made this festival possible. It's your vision that everyone is going to enjoy."

Dora felt a blush creeping up her cheeks. "Thanks. But still, I appreciate you being there to keep me grounded."

As they continued to set up, the atmosphere around them pulsed with energy. Laughter rang out from nearby booths where volunteers were preparing decorations, and children dashed around, their giggles filling the crisp evening air. It was a stark contrast to the tense atmosphere of the past weeks, and for the first time in a long while, Dora felt genuinely at ease.

"Hey, what do you say we take a break?" Oliver suggested, wiping sweat from his brow. "We've been at this for hours."

Dora nodded, grateful for the chance to step away from the bustle. "That sounds great. I could use a breather."

They found a quiet corner of the square, the soft glow of the lights illuminating their faces. They leaned against a wooden fence, watching the townsfolk rush about, excitement palpable in the air.

"Do you remember our first meeting?" Oliver asked, his eyes sparkling with mischief. "You were so intense about your ideas, I thought you might scare me off."

Dora laughed, a warm feeling bubbling up inside her. "I was a bit much, wasn't I? I just wanted to make sure the festival was perfect."

"It worked," he replied, his voice steady. "But I also admired your drive. Not everyone has that kind of passion."

"Thank you," she said, her gaze falling to the ground. "I guess I've always been this way. I just want to create something special for everyone."

"Why?" Oliver asked, his tone softening. "What's so important about it to you?"

Dora hesitated, the question striking a chord deep within her. "I suppose it's because I've always felt like an outsider in this town. I want to bring people together, to show them that there's beauty in our differences. I want to create a space where everyone feels welcome."

"Dora, you're not an outsider," Oliver said gently. "You've brought so much to this town. The festival is a testament to that. You're creating something memorable for everyone, including yourself."

His words resonated with her, and for a moment, she was lost in the warmth of his gaze. There was a sincerity in his eyes that made her heart flutter. "I guess I just hope it means something to the community. That it can bridge the gaps and create lasting memories."

"I think it will," Oliver assured her, his voice laced with conviction. "And you'll be the one at the center of it all, making it happen. You deserve to be celebrated too."

Dora felt a swell of emotion welling up inside her, her heart racing at his compliment. She wanted to reach out, to bridge that invisible gap that had formed between them. "And you? What about you? Why are you so invested in this?"

Oliver's smile faltered slightly, a flicker of vulnerability passing over his face. "I guess it's because I've been through a lot in my life. I've always felt like I needed to prove something, to myself and others. I want to make an impact, to be part of something that matters."

Dora nodded, understanding his words all too well. "You're doing that. You're making a difference. I see how hard you've worked, how much you care."

The moment hung between them, charged with unspoken feelings. Dora could feel the warmth radiating from Oliver, the air around them thick with anticipation. For a brief second, time seemed to stand still, and the world around them faded into the background.

"Dora," Oliver said, his voice low. "I—"

Before he could finish, a loud crash interrupted them. They both jumped, breaking the tension as they turned to see one of the decorations toppling over in the wind. Laughter erupted from nearby volunteers as they rushed to fix it, and Dora felt the moment slip away.

"Guess we should get back to it," Oliver said, his tone suddenly light. But there was a hint of disappointment in his eyes that tugged at Dora's heart.

"Yeah, we should," she replied, forcing a smile. "Let's make this festival one to remember."

As they rejoined the chaos of preparation, Dora couldn't shake the feeling of what had almost happened. She felt a connection with Oliver that was deeper than friendship, but the fear of what that meant held her back. Would it complicate their partnership? Would it change everything they had built?

They worked side by side into the night, the twinkling lights illuminating their path as they navigated the final touches of the festival. But the electric tension lingered in the air, each shared glance and lingering touch weaving a thread of unacknowledged feelings between them.

Chapter 11: A Mysterious Stranger

The sun rose over Winterhaven, casting a soft glow on the freshly decorated town square. Excitement filled the air as vendors set up their booths, and laughter erupted from children darting between stalls. Dora stood at the edge of the square, watching the festival come to life with a sense of pride. Everything they had worked for was finally taking shape.

Oliver joined her, a cup of hot cocoa in hand. "Can you believe it? It's happening!" he said, his eyes sparkling with enthusiasm.

"Finally!" Dora replied, her heart racing with anticipation. "It looks incredible. I can't wait for everyone to arrive."

Just then, a tall figure caught her eye. A man in a dark coat strolled into the square, his presence commanding attention. He had an air of mystery about him, his face partially obscured by the collar of his coat. Dora felt a strange tug of curiosity as he surveyed the scene, his gaze lingering on the various decorations and the gathering crowd.

"Who's that?" Oliver asked, following her line of sight. "I haven't seen him around before."

"I don't know," Dora replied, frowning slightly. "He doesn't look familiar at all. Something about him feels... off."

Before they could speculate further, the man approached one of the booths selling handmade ornaments. He examined the crafts with a discerning eye, nodding in approval before turning to the vendor. Dora's instincts tingled with unease as she watched him engage in conversation.

"Should we check it out?" Oliver suggested, his tone lighthearted, but Dora could sense an underlying tension.

"Let's give it a minute," she said, her intuition urging caution. "I don't want to jump to conclusions, but I just have this feeling."

As the festival continued to unfold, Dora tried to shake off the lingering unease. The square filled with families, laughter, and the smell of delicious treats. She and Oliver moved from booth to booth, soaking in the joy around them. However, the mysterious man remained in the back of her mind, his presence an unwelcome shadow.

Hours passed, and the festival was in full swing. The sound of music floated through the air, and the atmosphere buzzed with excitement. Just as Dora was beginning to relax, she spotted the stranger again. This time, he was near the main stage, talking to Evelyn.

Dora's heart raced as she felt an instinctive urge to intervene. "I don't like this," she whispered to Oliver, her voice tense. "We should go over there."

"Let's see what's happening first," he replied, his brow furrowed in thought. "Maybe he's just a visitor."

But as they drew closer, Dora could see the expression on Evelyn's face—concern mixed with confusion. The stranger gestured animatedly, his voice low, and Dora felt a knot forming in her stomach.

"Evelyn!" Dora called, waving her hand to get her attention. "Is everything okay?"

Evelyn turned, relief flooding her features as she saw them. "Dora! Oliver! Thank goodness you're here. This is—"

"Victor," the man interjected, his voice smooth and confident. "I'm just passing through. I heard about your festival and wanted to see it for myself."

"What brings you to Winterhaven?" Oliver asked, his tone polite but cautious.

"I'm an event organizer," Victor replied, his eyes glinting with interest. "I've worked on festivals and gatherings all over the country. I couldn't resist checking out this one."

Dora felt a flicker of skepticism. "That's great, but what's your interest in our festival?"

Victor smiled, a hint of mischief in his eyes. "I see potential here. You have something special, but it could be even bigger. I could help you elevate it."

Evelyn frowned. "We appreciate your interest, but we've worked hard to plan this festival ourselves. We don't need outside help."

"Of course, I understand," Victor said smoothly, but his gaze remained fixed on Dora and Oliver. "I'm not suggesting you need my help. I'm merely offering my expertise, should you ever want to expand beyond this year."

Dora crossed her arms, feeling defensive. "We're focused on this festival for now. We don't want to dilute what we've created."

Victor's smile widened, but there was something unsettling about it. "I admire your dedication. Just keep me in mind if you ever reconsider. You never know when a bit of fresh perspective might be useful."

With that, he turned and walked away, disappearing into the crowd. Dora felt a chill run down her spine. She glanced at Oliver, who shared her concern.

"What do you think?" Oliver asked, his voice low. "Was that just harmless chatter?"

"I don't know, but I didn't like how he looked at the festival," Dora replied, her instincts screaming at her. "He seemed too interested in how we could improve things, and I don't like the idea of someone wanting to change what we've built."

"I get it," Oliver said, his brow furrowing. "But maybe he was just being friendly. We can't let it ruin our day. Let's focus on the festival."

Dora nodded, but unease lingered in her chest. As they moved through the festival, the joy around them felt overshadowed by Victor's presence. She couldn't shake the feeling that he was more than just an event organizer passing through.

As night fell, the festival transformed. The lights glimmered like stars, and the sounds of laughter echoed throughout the square. It was a beautiful sight, yet Dora felt a gnawing anxiety in her gut. She had a growing suspicion that Victor was up to something, and it was distracting her from the joy of the night.

Just before the light show began, Dora and Oliver stood at the front of the stage, the crowd buzzing with anticipation. As the lights began to flicker and dance, illuminating the square in a breathtaking display, Dora caught sight of Victor again, standing at the edge of the crowd, his expression unreadable.

"Oliver," she whispered, her voice barely audible above the music. "Look."

Oliver turned, his gaze narrowing. "What is he doing?"

"I don't know, but it's like he's waiting for something," she replied, feeling a sense of urgency. "I don't like this. We should keep an eye on him."

As the light show erupted in a stunning spectacle of colors, Dora felt a momentary thrill. But her eyes remained fixed on Victor. The excitement of the festival swirled around her, yet she couldn't fully immerse herself in it, her instincts still on high alert.

Suddenly, a loud bang echoed through the square, shattering the enchanting atmosphere. Dora's heart raced as she turned to see flames erupting from one of the nearby stalls. Panic erupted in the crowd, and chaos ensued. People screamed and scattered, and Dora's heart sank.

"Dora!" Oliver shouted over the noise. "We need to help!"

Without hesitation, they rushed toward the stall, adrenaline coursing through their veins. Dora's mind raced with fear as she fought to stay focused. The flames grew larger, and the nearby stalls were in danger.

"Get the fire extinguisher!" Oliver shouted, searching for anything that could help.

Dora spotted a bucket of water nearby and grabbed it, hurling its contents onto the flames, but it barely made a dent. The heat intensified, and she felt the heat on her skin.

Victor appeared out of nowhere, rushing to the front of the stall. "Everyone, step back!" he commanded, his voice carrying through the chaos. "I can help!"

Dora felt a surge of anger. "What are you doing? We don't need your help!"

But as he moved closer, he revealed a fire extinguisher he had pulled from a nearby booth. "Trust me! I can put this out!"

Dora hesitated but then nodded, realizing they needed all the help they could get. Victor sprayed the extinguisher with a practiced hand, and the flames began to subside. The crowd watched, a mix of fear and awe on their faces.

After a few tense moments, the flames finally extinguished, leaving the stall charred and smoking. The crowd erupted into relieved applause, but Dora's heart was still racing.

"Are you okay?" Oliver asked, checking her for injuries.

"I think so," she replied, her voice shaky. "But what just happened? Why did that happen?"

Victor stood nearby, catching his breath, but the triumphant smile on his face made her uneasy. "That was a close call," he said, his tone casual. "You handled that well. But you should really be more prepared for these kinds of things."

Dora narrowed her eyes at him, suspicion bubbling beneath the surface. "You were standing there, waiting for something to happen, weren't you?"

Victor's smile faltered slightly, but he quickly masked it. "I was simply observing, as any good organizer would. You never know when an emergency might arise. It's always best to be prepared."

"Prepared for what?" she challenged, anger flaring in her chest. "You think you can just swoop in and take over? This is our festival!"

Oliver stepped between them, sensing the tension. "Dora, let's not escalate things. We need to focus on the aftermath of this."

Dora shook her head, her emotions running high. "I won't let him manipulate this festival. We've worked too hard for it."

Victor raised his hands in mock surrender. "I'm not here to take over. I'm just offering my assistance, but I can see that you're very protective of your vision."

As he spoke, Dora felt a sense of unease settle over her. She knew there was more to Victor than he let on, and she couldn't shake the feeling that he was lurking in the shadows for a reason.

"Let's get the crowd settled," Oliver suggested, trying to diffuse the situation. "We can't let this ruin the festival."

Dora nodded, but her thoughts were racing. They had fought so hard to create something special, and now it felt like they were being undermined. As the chaos began to settle, Dora knew one thing for sure: she wouldn't let Victor disrupt their hard work.

Chapter 12: Unlikely Allies

As the smoke from the extinguished flames began to clear, Dora felt the weight of the day's events pressing down on her. The festival, once a symbol of hope and celebration, now seemed tainted by Victor's interference. With the crowd beginning to disperse and the excitement dampened, Dora and Oliver knew they had to act quickly.

"Dora, we can't let him ruin everything we've worked for," Oliver said, his tone resolute. "We need to keep an eye on him."

"Agreed," she replied, glancing over her shoulder to see Victor chatting with a group of festival-goers, his demeanor casual, as if the chaos earlier had never happened. "He's too interested in what we're doing, and I don't trust him."

They exchanged a determined look, both understanding the urgency of the situation. "What's our plan?" Oliver asked, rubbing the back of his neck as he surveyed the square, now littered with remnants of the day's excitement.

"First, we need to gather information about him," Dora suggested. "We need to find out who he really is and what he wants. If we can catch him off guard, maybe we can uncover his intentions."

"Okay," Oliver said, nodding in agreement. "Let's split up. I'll talk to some of the vendors and see if anyone has heard of him. You keep an eye on him from a distance. Try to see if he's talking to anyone else of interest."

Dora hesitated, feeling a flicker of doubt. "Are you sure it's safe? What if he catches on to what we're doing?"

Oliver smiled reassuringly. "I'll be careful. Besides, it's not like we have much of a choice. We can't let him undermine our hard work."

With a nod, they set their plan in motion. Dora moved toward the edge of the square, staying within sight of Victor, who was now engaged in conversation with another vendor. She discreetly pulled out her phone, scrolling through social media to see if there were any recent mentions of him. Meanwhile, Oliver began mingling with the vendors, casually asking about Victor without raising suspicion.

As Dora observed Victor, she noted his charm and how effortlessly he interacted with others. He was clearly skilled at making people feel at ease, a talent that both fascinated and unnerved her. What was he really after?

Suddenly, her phone buzzed. It was a message from Oliver.

"I talked to one of the vendors. They said Victor has been around the area for a while but hasn't

worked on any major events. Something feels off."

Dora's heart raced. "He's a mystery we need to solve," she muttered to herself. Just as she was about to reply, she noticed Victor moving away from the crowd, heading toward a quieter section of the square.

"Where are you going?" she whispered, following him at a safe distance.

Victor strolled past the remnants of the festival, stopping at a secluded corner behind a row of booths. He pulled out his phone and began typing furiously. Dora squinted, trying to get a better look, but the angle was difficult.

Suddenly, she heard Oliver's voice behind her. "Dora! Over here!" He waved her over, his expression serious. "I just found something."

Dora hesitated, torn between staying on Victor's trail and following Oliver. The urgency in his voice won her over. She quickly made her way back to him, her heart racing with anticipation.

"What did you find?" she asked, her breath catching in her throat.

"I spoke with someone who recognized Victor," Oliver said, lowering his voice. "They said he used to work in event planning, but something happened—something that made him leave town under suspicious circumstances."

"Like what?" Dora pressed, her curiosity piqued.

"I couldn't get all the details," Oliver admitted, glancing around to ensure they were not overheard. "But it sounds like he might have been involved in some shady dealings. No one wants to talk about it."

Dora felt a surge of adrenaline. "That explains why he's here. He's looking for a fresh start, and it's likely he wants to manipulate this festival for his own gain."

"Exactly," Oliver said, his eyes narrowing in determination. "We need to find out more about his past. Maybe we can get some of the other vendors on our side to help gather intel."

Dora nodded, her mind racing. "Let's talk to Evelyn. She knows everyone in town and might have heard something."

As they headed toward the main stage where Evelyn was checking on the decorations, Dora's heart raced with the thrill of their newfound mission. They needed to act fast before Victor could enact whatever plan he had in mind.

Evelyn was busy fixing a few ornaments that had fallen during the chaos of the earlier fire. When she saw them approaching, she straightened up, wiping her hands on her apron. "How's it going? I heard about the fire; that was scary!"

Dora exchanged a glance with Oliver before speaking. "We need to talk about Victor. Have you heard anything about him?"

Evelyn's brow furrowed in thought. "I saw him earlier. He seemed nice enough, but I did get a strange vibe from him. Why?"

Dora explained what they had learned from the vendor and their suspicions about Victor's intentions. Evelyn listened carefully, nodding as they spoke.

"I had my reservations about him too," she admitted. "He seemed too eager to offer help, and I didn't like the way he was eyeing the festival. If he's had a questionable past, we need to keep an eye on him."

"Exactly," Oliver said. "We think he might be trying to undermine our efforts. Do you have any connections that could help us dig deeper into his background?"

Evelyn thought for a moment before nodding. "I can reach out to a few people who know more about the town's history. If he's been around here for a while, someone might know what happened."

"Thank you, Evelyn," Dora said, feeling a wave of gratitude. "We need all the help we can get."

As Evelyn made calls, Dora and Oliver brainstormed how they could protect the festival while keeping tabs on Victor. They decided to keep a close watch on him, hoping to gather enough evidence to confront him if necessary.

"Let's meet back here in an hour," Oliver suggested, glancing at the dwindling crowd. "If anything feels off, we can strategize on how to deal with it."

"Sounds good," Dora replied, her resolve solidifying. "We're not going to let him take away what we've built. This festival is for our community, and we'll do whatever it takes to protect it."

With their plan in motion, they split up again, Dora watching Victor while Oliver sought out information. The tension in the air hung thick as Dora kept her distance, her heart pounding as she waited for the right moment to confront him.

Chapter 13: Confrontation

The sun dipped lower in the sky, casting a golden glow over the remnants of the festival. As the excitement slowly dissipated, Dora felt a growing urgency. She had to confront Victor before he could enact any more of his plans. The weight of their suspicions hung heavily on her, and she refused to let fear dictate her actions.

Finding Oliver amidst the bustle of cleanup, she caught his eye. "We need to talk to Victor now," she said, her voice steady but her heart racing.

Oliver frowned. "Are you sure that's wise? He might not react well."

Dora squared her shoulders, determination flooding her veins. "We can't let him think he has the upper hand. If we confront him, we might uncover the truth and stop him before he causes more damage."

Oliver nodded, sensing the fire in her resolve. "Okay. Let's find him."

They began scanning the square, but Victor seemed to have vanished from sight. Dora felt a flicker of anxiety. "Where did he go?"

"Let's check near the vendor area," Oliver suggested. "He might be trying to gather information or recruit someone to help him."

They made their way toward the cluster of booths, keeping their eyes peeled for Victor. As they approached, Dora noticed a small group of vendors gathered, their expressions tense as they whispered among themselves.

"There he is," Oliver muttered, nodding toward Victor, who stood at the edge of the group, animatedly talking to a vendor named Marcus.

Dora's breath quickened. "Now's our chance."

With Oliver at her side, she approached Victor, her heart pounding in her chest. As they drew closer, Victor caught sight of them and a sly smile crept onto his face.

"Dora, Oliver! Just the people I wanted to see," he said, his tone dripping with feigned warmth. "How's the festival treating you?"

"Cut the small talk, Victor," Dora said, her voice firm. "We need to talk about your intentions."

Victor raised an eyebrow, feigning innocence. "My intentions? I'm just here to help, of course."

"Help?" Oliver interjected, crossing his arms. "By causing chaos? You have a funny way of showing it."

Victor's demeanor shifted slightly, and Dora noticed a flicker of irritation in his eyes. "You're mistaken. I was merely trying to bring some excitement to the festival."

"Excitement?" Dora pressed, her frustration mounting. "You set fire to our decorations and tried to disrupt everything we've worked for!"

Victor chuckled, a sound devoid of any real humor. "It was an accident, I assure you. But if you're so concerned, maybe it's time to consider that not everyone has your best interests at heart."

"What does that mean?" Oliver demanded, stepping closer to Victor. "Are you threatening us?"

"Not at all," Victor replied smoothly, but the glint in his eyes suggested otherwise. "I simply mean that some people have a knack for drawing attention, even when it's unintentional. You might want to look over your shoulders."

Dora felt a chill run down her spine, but she refused to show any fear. "We're not afraid of you, Victor. If you think you can intimidate us, you're wrong."

"Oh, I'm not trying to intimidate," he said, leaning in slightly, his voice low and conspiratorial. "I'm merely pointing out that the world is much larger than you think. And I happen to have a few connections that could make your lives... complicated."

Before Dora could respond, the murmurs from the group of vendors grew louder, and Marcus stepped forward, his face pale. "Victor, you don't have to threaten them. We all know what happened in the past."

Victor's expression darkened. "What past are you referring to, Marcus?"

"The one that got you run out of town," Marcus replied, voice trembling slightly. "We don't want that kind of trouble here."

Dora's heart raced at the revelation. "What do you mean?" she asked, glancing between Victor and Marcus.

Victor's facade cracked, revealing a glimpse of the man beneath. "That was a long time ago," he said, but there was an edge to his tone. "I've changed."

"Changed?" Oliver scoffed. "You're clearly up to something. You think we're going to just let you walk away?"

With tension mounting, Dora realized they had an opportunity. "We need to know what happened, Victor. If you're really here to help, then prove it. Tell us about your past and why you're really here."

Victor's eyes narrowed, and for a moment, it seemed as though he might refuse. But then he seemed to reconsider, a smirk returning to his lips. "Fine, I'll indulge you," he said. "But know that some truths are better left buried."

As he began to speak, the vendors leaned in, curiosity and apprehension etched on their faces.

"I was involved in event planning in a neighboring town," Victor began, his voice smooth yet filled with an underlying tension. "Things started well, but as the events grew in scale, so did the competition. I made some enemies, and accusations started flying—some justified, some not. In the end, it didn't matter. I was the scapegoat, and I was forced to leave."

"Is that what you call it?" Marcus cut in, his voice rising. "You didn't just leave; you were chased out. Everyone knows you were involved in sabotaging other events to ensure your own success."

Victor bristled, his charming mask slipping once again. "Those are just rumors! I was trying to make a name for myself. I was passionate about what I did. And now you all act like I'm some sort of monster."

Dora felt the room shift, the tension hanging heavy in the air. "You didn't answer our question, Victor. What do you want with this festival? What do you hope to gain?"

He paused, his expression unreadable. "I want what everyone wants—success, recognition. But I have to admit, I also enjoy the thrill of the game."

"That's not good enough," Oliver said, taking a step closer. "We won't let you ruin our hard work for your amusement. You need to leave."

Victor chuckled softly, almost mockingly. "You really think you can just order me away? You're in over your heads. This festival is just the beginning; I could bring it down in an instant if I wanted."

Dora felt her heart race with anger. "You're playing a dangerous game, Victor. You think we're afraid of you? We'll expose you if we have to."

"Expose me?" Victor sneered. "Good luck with that. You don't know the half of it. I have friends in high places. You're nothing but a small-town event planner, and I can make your lives a nightmare."

"Enough!" a voice called out, cutting through the tension like a knife. It was Evelyn, stepping forward with an air of authority. "You're not going to threaten my friends here. We're all in this together, and we won't let you disrupt what we've built."

Dora felt a wave of relief wash over her. "Thank you, Evelyn," she said, grateful for her support.

Victor shot them both a glare, but the tension in his posture softened slightly. "You really think you can stand against me? I'll be watching, and you'll regret this."

With that, he turned and walked away, the crowd parting before him as if sensing the storm that had just passed. Dora felt her heart pound in her chest, adrenaline still coursing through her veins. They had confronted him, but the threat still loomed over the festival.

"Are you okay?" Oliver asked, concern etched on his face.

Dora took a deep breath, trying to steady herself. "I'm fine. But we can't let our guard down. He's not going to give up easily."

"I know," Oliver replied, glancing at the departing figure of Victor. "But at least we've shown him we're not afraid."

Dora nodded, her mind racing with the implications of their confrontation. They needed to regroup and prepare for whatever Victor had in store. This wasn't over yet, and the stakes were higher than ever.

Chapter 14: Victor's Revenge

The tension from the earlier confrontation hung thick in the air as Dora and Oliver regrouped. Their bravado during the encounter with Victor felt fleeting now, replaced by a sense of urgency. They needed to remain vigilant; Victor wouldn't take their defiance lightly.

As evening descended over the festival grounds, the once-vibrant atmosphere turned somber. The stalls that had brimmed with life just hours before now stood eerily quiet, remnants of the day's joy overshadowed by the threat Victor posed. Dora could feel the weight of every vendor's gaze upon her, their trust and hopes resting on her shoulders.

"We need to keep an eye on everything," Oliver said, scanning the area. "If he's going to do something, it'll likely be tonight or tomorrow when the festival is in full swing."

Dora nodded, determination flooding her veins. "Let's check the main stage and the area where the food vendors set up. If Victor has a plan, it could involve tampering with supplies or equipment."

As they moved through the fairgrounds, they were on high alert, every noise sending a jolt of adrenaline through their bodies. The vibrant decorations now felt like a disguise hiding potential chaos. They reached the main stage, its lights dimming as the last of the performers finished their rehearsals.

"Let's look around backstage," Oliver suggested, his voice low.

They slipped behind the curtain, where the sound of laughter echoed from the performers who were wrapping up their evening. The area was cluttered with equipment, but nothing seemed out of the ordinary. Dora began to relax until a sudden crash resonated from the food vendor area.

"Did you hear that?" Oliver asked, eyes wide.

Dora nodded, her heart racing again as they rushed toward the sound. As they approached, they saw a crowd gathered around the food stall, people shouting and panicking. The vibrant aromas that had once filled the air were replaced by smoke and confusion.

"What happened?" Dora shouted as she pushed her way through the crowd, Oliver right behind her.

One of the vendors, a woman named Clara, was standing by her booth, hands on her hips, looking furious. "It was sabotaged! The propane tanks—someone cut the safety line!"

Dora's stomach dropped. "Is anyone hurt?"

"Not yet," Clara replied, her voice trembling. "But if we hadn't noticed the smell of gas, it could have exploded! We need to alert everyone!"

Dora glanced at Oliver, who was already pulling out his phone. "I'll call the police. We need to file a report, and we need to make sure everyone is safe."

As Oliver dialed, Dora stepped closer to Clara. "Did you see anyone suspicious around here before it happened?"

Clara shook her head, frustration etched on her face. "No, it all happened so quickly. I just went to grab supplies and—"

"I think it was Victor," Dora interrupted, her mind racing. "He's been lurking around, and this has his fingerprints all over it."

Oliver ended his call and turned to them, his expression grave. "The police are on their way. We need to secure the area and ensure everyone is accounted for."

Dora nodded, adrenaline coursing through her veins. "Clara, can you gather the other vendors? We need to keep everyone informed and on high alert."

Clara nodded, already stepping away to rally the other vendors. As she did, Dora turned to Oliver.

"We need to warn the festival organizers. They need to know what's happening."

"I'll handle that," he said, moving to find the festival director.

With urgency surging within her, Dora decided to head back to the main square. She knew Victor wouldn't just stop there. He was bound to have more tricks up his sleeve. She needed to find him before he caused more chaos.

As she hurried through the fairgrounds, her mind raced with possibilities. What else could Victor do to undermine the festival? If he was this willing to sabotage their food supplies, what about the entertainment? The security of the entire event was at stake, and she couldn't allow fear to paralyze her.

Suddenly, she caught a glimpse of movement from the corner of her eye. It was Victor, sneaking behind one of the vendor tents. Her heart pounded, and she instinctively followed, her determination propelling her forward.

Dora edged closer, making sure to stay out of sight. She could hear Victor muttering to himself, his hands fiddling with something—a small device that glinted in the fading light.

"What are you up to?" she whispered to herself, her breath catching.

Taking a deep breath, she decided to confront him. "What are you doing, Victor?" she called out, stepping into the open.

He spun around, his face morphing from surprise to annoyance. "Dora," he said, feigning innocence. "What a pleasant surprise."

"Cut the act. I saw you back here. What are you planning?" She took a step closer, her eyes locked on the device in his hand. "If you think you can sabotage this festival, you're mistaken."

Victor smirked, a glint of menace flashing in his eyes. "And what are you going to do about it? You think you can stop me?"

"You're playing a dangerous game," she warned, her voice steady. "This festival isn't just an event; it's about our community. You don't belong here, and we won't let you destroy what we've built."

"Built?" Victor scoffed, his demeanor shifting. "This is all so fragile. One little push, and it all crumbles. Just like I've seen happen before."

"Is that what this is about?" Dora challenged, feeling anger bubble within her. "You want to prove something? You want revenge for something that happened in your past? This isn't just a game!"

Victor's expression darkened, and for a moment, the mask of charm slipped completely. "You think you understand me? You have no idea what I've sacrificed for this life. If you get in my way, I will ruin you. I will bring this whole festival crashing down."

Dora stood her ground, the weight of his threats heavy upon her. "You're making a mistake. You don't have to do this. We can find a way to work together—"

"Work together?" He laughed, a cold, harsh sound. "You're naive, Dora. The world doesn't work that way. You can't change what I am."

Before she could respond, Victor turned away, seemingly uninterested. But as he did, Dora spotted the device he had been holding—a small canister marked with a warning label.

"Victor, wait!" she shouted, rushing forward.

But it was too late. Victor took off running, disappearing into the shadows of the festival grounds.

"Damn it!" Dora cursed, frustration bubbling over. She quickly picked up the canister he had dropped, the warning label clearly indicating that it was a chemical intended for use in fireworks.

"Oliver!" she called out, her voice urgent. "I need you!"

Oliver rushed into view, his expression filled with concern. "What's wrong?"

"He was here," she said, holding up the canister. "Victor was trying to tamper with the fireworks for the finale. If we don't stop him, it could be disastrous."

"What do we do?" Oliver asked, his brow furrowed with determination.

"We alert everyone. We need to shut down the fireworks until we can confirm they're safe," she replied, her mind racing with possibilities. "And we need to find Victor before he can carry out whatever plan he has."

Together, they raced back toward the main square, adrenaline surging through them as they prepared to confront Victor and protect their festival from his malicious intent.

Chapter 15: Alerting the Crowd

The vibrant atmosphere of the festival felt suffocating as Dora and Oliver rushed back toward the main square, the weight of urgency pressing on their shoulders. The joyous sounds of laughter and celebration echoed around them, oblivious to the chaos that was brewing just beneath the surface.

"Oliver, we need to make sure everyone understands the danger we're facing," Dora said, her heart pounding. "If Victor's plan goes through, it could hurt a lot of people."

"I know. Let's find Evelyn and the festival committee. They need to know what's at stake," Oliver replied, his brow furrowed with determination.

They quickly navigated through the throngs of festival-goers, the colorful lights and festive decorations creating a stark contrast to the seriousness of their mission. As they approached the main stage, they spotted Evelyn talking to a group of vendors. She looked relieved to see them.

"Dora! Oliver! Thank goodness you're back. What's going on?" Evelyn asked, her eyes searching their faces.

"Victor is sabotaging the festival," Dora said, her voice steady despite the rising panic within her. "He was back at the food vendor area trying to cut the safety lines on the propane tanks. We think he's also tampering with the fireworks."

Evelyn's expression hardened. "What do you mean?"

Dora held up the canister Victor had dropped, the warning label clearly visible. "This is what he was using. It's a chemical intended for fireworks. If we don't shut down the display, it could be catastrophic."

Evelyn's eyes widened as she took in the gravity of the situation. "We need to warn everyone. If he's already set things in motion, we don't have much time."

Dora nodded. "We have to act fast. We can't let Victor disrupt this festival any further."

"Let's gather everyone," Evelyn said, her voice rising as she turned to the crowd. "Everyone, may I have your attention, please! We need to talk about the safety of tonight's fireworks display!"

The crowd began to quiet, the excited chatter replaced by murmurs of confusion. Dora watched as familiar faces turned toward them, curiosity and concern etched in their expressions.

"There's been a security issue regarding the fireworks," Evelyn continued, her voice steady. "We believe someone has tampered with the equipment, and for everyone's safety, we're postponing the display until we can ensure it's secure."

"Postponing? What do you mean?" a voice called out from the crowd, a vendor named Henry. "We've been looking forward to this all year!"

"I understand your frustration," Evelyn replied, maintaining her composure. "But our priority is everyone's safety. We can't risk an accident."

A chorus of voices began to rise, some arguing against the decision while others expressed agreement. Dora felt the tension in the air, the stakes climbing higher with each passing moment.

"Everyone, please listen!" Dora called out, stepping forward. "Victor is a threat to this festival. He's already tried to sabotage the food vendors, and we believe he has plans for the fireworks. We cannot take any chances."

The crowd shifted, whispers and concerned looks spreading among them. "What do you suggest we do?" asked Clara, the vendor who had alerted them to the food sabotage. "If he's out there, he could strike again."

Evelyn nodded, her eyes narrowing with resolve. "We need to secure the area. If we can keep everyone together and watch each other's backs, we might be able to catch him in the act."

"Dora and I can patrol the area," Oliver suggested. "If we split into teams and watch the entrances, we can keep an eye out for anything suspicious."

"That's a good idea," Evelyn said, her expression firm. "Clara, can you help rally the other vendors to set up a watch around the main square? And the rest of you, stay alert and keep your eyes open."

Dora felt a surge of hope. "If we work together, we can keep everyone safe and prevent Victor from ruining this festival."

As the crowd dispersed into small groups, ready to mobilize, Dora and Oliver moved to the edge of the square, scanning the area for any signs of Victor. The festive lights flickered overhead, casting a surreal glow on the scene.

"I can't believe he would go this far," Oliver said, his eyes narrowed in determination. "He's willing to hurt people just to prove a point."

"We can't let him win," Dora replied, steeling herself. "We need to find him and make sure he doesn't get a chance to carry out his plans."

They decided to split up to cover more ground. "I'll check the vendor area again," Oliver said. "You take the path toward the outskirts of the festival. If he's trying to blend in, he might be hiding in plain sight."

"Be careful," Dora warned, feeling a rush of concern for her friend. "If you see him, don't confront him alone."

"Same to you," Oliver replied, giving her a reassuring nod before heading off into the bustling crowd.

As Dora made her way through the festival, she kept her senses sharp, searching for any sign of Victor. The joyful atmosphere around her felt increasingly strained, and her heart raced at the thought of what could happen if they didn't act quickly.

She moved toward the outskirts, where the festivities were quieter. As she turned a corner, she spotted a shadowy figure lingering near the edge of the carnival games. Her heart raced as she recognized the familiar outline—Victor.

"Victor!" she called out, her voice ringing with authority. "Stop right there!"

He turned, a wicked smile spreading across his face as he took a step back into the shadows. "Dora, always so eager to play the hero. But you're too late."

Dora felt a rush of adrenaline, anger boiling within her. "What do you want, Victor? Are you really willing to hurt people just to satisfy your ego?"

He chuckled softly, the sound echoing through the quiet night. "It's not about satisfaction, dear. It's about proving a point. This festival is a façade, and I intend to expose it for what it really is—a weak little celebration doomed to fail."

"By putting lives at risk?" Dora pressed, stepping closer. "That's not a point worth making."

Victor tilted his head, mock concern etched on his face. "Oh, but don't you see? It's the only way to make them realize how fragile it all is. One spark, and it all comes crumbling down."

Dora took a deep breath, her voice steady as she replied, "You don't have to do this. You can choose to walk away and leave us alone."

"But where's the fun in that?" Victor retorted, his grin widening. "You think you can stop me? I've already set the wheels in motion."

"What do you mean?" Dora demanded, fear creeping into her voice.

He stepped back into the shadows, his figure fading from view. "Let's just say the fireworks are about to become much more interesting. Enjoy the show, Dora."

Before she could react, he disappeared, leaving her standing in the dim light of the festival. Panic surged through her as she realized what he meant. The fireworks were still scheduled to go off, and Victor was out there, poised to carry out his plan.

"Oliver!" she shouted, her voice echoing in the night. "We have to stop him!"

Chapter 16: Unexpected Help

Dora's heart raced as she stood alone in the dim light of the festival grounds, panic rising within her. Victor was out there, plotting something catastrophic, and time was running out. She needed to act quickly, but she couldn't do it alone.

Just as she turned to head back to the main square, she noticed a familiar figure approaching from the shadows. It was Clara, the food vendor who had been instrumental in sounding the alarm earlier.

"Dora! I was looking for you!" Clara called out, her expression a mix of concern and determination. "I overheard something that might help us."

Dora felt a surge of hope. "What did you hear?"

"I was talking to some of the other vendors after you left, and we started discussing our suspicions about Victor. One of them mentioned seeing him meeting with someone behind the fairground earlier today. They were acting secretive, like they were planning something," Clara explained, her voice urgent.

Dora's mind raced. "Do you know who he was meeting with?"

"No, but they were definitely plotting something. It seemed like they were discussing the fireworks. I think they might have some sort of inside knowledge about how they're set up," Clara replied.

"Then we have to find out what they're planning!" Dora exclaimed, feeling a new sense of urgency. "Do you know where they were?"

Clara nodded, her expression resolute. "I can show you the spot. If we hurry, we might catch them before they leave."

"Let's go!" Dora urged, and together, they moved through the festival grounds, the vibrant lights dimming in the backdrop of their rising dread.

As they made their way toward the edge of the festival, Clara pointed to a small area behind one of the food stalls. "They were talking over there, near the loading dock. It's usually quiet, away from the festivities."

Dora's heart raced as they approached the spot, her mind racing with possibilities. If Victor had help, it could complicate their efforts to stop him. "We need to be careful," she whispered. "We don't know who else might be involved."

As they neared the loading dock, Clara motioned for Dora to crouch low behind a stack of crates. "Let's see if we can overhear anything."

They settled behind the crates, peering around the corner. A flickering light illuminated the area, and Dora's heart sank as she caught sight of Victor, flanked by a tall figure with a hood pulled low over their face.

"Are you sure everything is set?" Victor asked, his tone low and serious. "We can't afford any mistakes."

The other person nodded, their voice muffled. "I've got everything under control. The fireworks will go off as planned, but we need to act quickly. If anyone gets in the way, it could ruin everything."

Dora exchanged a worried glance with Clara. This was worse than they had feared. "We need to find out what the plan is," she whispered urgently. "Do you have your phone? We need to record this."

Clara nodded, quickly pulling out her phone. She discreetly switched it to record, and they focused on the conversation unfolding before them.

"I don't care what it takes," Victor continued. "We need to show them that their little festival is nothing compared to the chaos I can create. They think they can just push me out? Let them see what I can really do."

The other figure laughed, a low, chilling sound. "And once they see, they'll never forget. Just make sure to stick to the plan."

Dora felt a shiver run down her spine. "We have to do something now," she whispered. "If we don't stop them, they'll ruin everything."

Clara looked at her, determination lighting her eyes. "You're right. We need to confront them and expose what they're planning."

Dora hesitated for a moment, then nodded. "Okay. We'll catch them off guard. Let's move in, and we'll figure out how to stop this together."

With her heart pounding in her chest, Dora and Clara quietly crept closer, inching toward Victor and his accomplice. Just as they were about to step into the light, Clara stumbled slightly, causing a soft thud against the crate.

The figures turned sharply, their expressions shifting from confidence to surprise.

"Who's there?" Victor barked, his eyes narrowing as he scanned the shadows.

"Run!" Dora shouted, pushing Clara to retreat as they both dashed away from the loading dock, their hearts racing.

They didn't stop until they reached the safety of the festival's main square, breathless and shaken.

"What do we do now?" Clara asked, her voice shaky.

"We need to tell Evelyn and Oliver what we overheard," Dora replied, urgency propelling her forward. "If they know Victor is planning to sabotage the fireworks, they can take action before it's too late."

As they approached the main stage, Dora spotted Oliver speaking with Evelyn and a group of concerned vendors. She rushed over, grabbing their attention.

"Oliver! Evelyn!" she called out, her voice rising above the noise of the crowd. "We have crucial information about Victor."

"What is it?" Oliver asked, his eyes narrowing in concern.

"Clara and I just overheard him talking to someone about the fireworks," Dora said, breathless. "They're planning to make it a disaster. We need to act fast before it's too late."

Evelyn's expression shifted to one of urgency. "We need to shut down the fireworks entirely. If they're plotting something, we can't take any chances."

"We should evacuate the area," Oliver added. "Get everyone away from the fireworks staging area until we know it's safe."

Dora nodded, her resolve strengthening. "Clara, can you help spread the word among the vendors? We need to make sure everyone knows what's going on."

"Of course!" Clara replied, determination lighting her features. "I'll make sure everyone stays clear."

As Clara rushed off, Dora turned to Evelyn and Oliver. "We need to find out who that accomplice was. If Victor has someone on the inside, it could complicate everything."

"Let's split up," Oliver suggested. "I'll check the other vendors and see if anyone recognizes them. You and Evelyn can secure the area and ensure the crowd is informed."

"Good idea," Dora agreed. "We'll meet back here in a short while."

They quickly split up, Dora's mind racing as she took in the festival surroundings, now filled with tension. She could see vendors packing up their goods, the festive atmosphere dimming in the face of the impending danger.

As she and Evelyn began to alert the festival-goers, Dora kept her eyes peeled for any sign of Victor or his accomplice. She could feel the weight of responsibility pressing down on her. The safety of the community was in her hands, and she couldn't let fear stop her from taking action.

"Everyone, may I have your attention, please!" Evelyn called out, her voice cutting through the murmur of the crowd. "We need to inform you of a serious situation regarding tonight's fireworks display. For your safety, we are postponing the show until we can ensure it is secure."

The crowd buzzed with confusion and concern, but Dora pressed on, her voice steady. "Please, stay calm. We're working to address the situation and will keep you updated. Your safety is our top priority."

Just as Dora turned to Evelyn to discuss their next steps, she caught sight of a figure lingering at the edge of the festival grounds. A hooded silhouette, eerily familiar.

"Evelyn, I think that's them!" Dora exclaimed, pointing toward the figure. "We need to find out who they are!"

Without waiting for a response, she started toward the figure, her heart pounding with determination. The festival lights flickered above her, casting an uncertain glow as she drew closer.

"Hey! You!" Dora called out, her voice steady despite the adrenaline coursing through her veins. "Stop right there!"

The figure froze, then slowly turned to face her, the hood slipping back to reveal a young man she had never seen before.

"What do you want?" he asked, a mix of defiance and fear in his voice.

"Who are you? Are you working with Victor?" Dora demanded, her instincts on high alert.

"Me? No! I—" he stammered, glancing around nervously. "I'm just here for the festival."

Dora narrowed her eyes, skepticism flooding her thoughts. "Then why were you with him?"

The young man looked panicked, glancing back toward the festival square. "I didn't know what he was planning! He just said to meet him here. I thought it was just for the fireworks."

"Why should I believe you?" Dora pressed, her voice firm.

"Because I don't want any part of this!" he exclaimed, desperation creeping into his tone. "I just wanted to see the show. I don't know what he's doing!"

Dora exchanged a glance with Evelyn, who stepped forward, her authority evident. "Then you need to help us. If you know anything, it's important."

"Fine," the young man said, his shoulders slumping in defeat. "I saw him earlier today, talking about how he wanted to make a statement. He was obsessed with ruining the festival."

"Do you know where he is now?" Evelyn pressed.

"He said something about the control room for the fireworks," the young man replied, his voice trembling. "I can show you. But you have to promise to keep me safe."

Dora nodded, her resolve hardening. "Lead the way."

As they began to move toward the fireworks control room, Dora's mind raced with possibilities. They were one step closer to stopping Victor, and she wouldn't let this opportunity slip away.

Chapter 17: The Race Against Time

Dora's heart thundered in her chest as she followed the young man, whose name she still didn't know, through the winding paths of the festival. Evelyn remained close behind, her determination radiating like a beacon. They had to reach the control room before Victor could execute his plan.

As they navigated through the festival's bustling crowds, the atmosphere shifted from festive excitement to a tense urgency. The vibrant lights flickered around them, creating shadows that seemed to loom larger as they approached the designated area for the fireworks setup.

"Is it far?" Dora asked, trying to keep her voice steady despite the adrenaline surging through her.

"Just around the corner," the young man replied, glancing nervously over his shoulder. "But you have to hurry. He said he wanted to surprise everyone, to make it a big spectacle. I don't know when he plans to set them off."

Dora's stomach twisted at the thought. If Victor was planning to set off the fireworks prematurely, it could lead to chaos, injuries, or worse. They had to get there fast.

"Do you have a key or anything to get us inside?" Evelyn asked, her voice calm and authoritative.

The young man shook his head. "No, but I know how to bypass the security measures. We just need to act quickly."

"Lead the way," Dora urged, determination flooding her.

They rounded the corner, coming upon a tall, fenced-in area where the fireworks were stored, a small building nestled against the edge of the fairground. The control room was located at the back, the door tightly shut, the dim light spilling from beneath it a stark reminder of the danger inside.

"Over here," the young man whispered, pointing to a side door that appeared to lead directly into the control room. "I can pick the lock, but we need to keep quiet."

Dora nodded, her pulse racing. "Do it."

He knelt down, fumbling with the lock. As he worked, Dora glanced around, scanning the area for any signs of Victor or his accomplice. The anticipation in the air felt thick, almost suffocating, as they waited.

"I think I heard them talking just before you showed up," he said, still focused on the lock. "They mentioned something about 'detonating early.'"

Dora felt a wave of dread wash over her. They were running out of time. "How long do you think we have?" she asked, her voice a mere whisper.

"Not long. They could set them off any minute," he replied, finally hearing a soft click as the lock turned.

"Got it!" he exclaimed, pushing the door open slowly, his breath coming out in a rush.

They slipped inside the small, dimly lit control room, filled with an array of equipment and blinking lights. Dora's heart sank as she took in the sight. It was exactly as she feared—Victor was already here, hunched over the control panel, his accomplice standing beside him, a glint of something metallic in their hand.

"Quick!" Dora hissed. "We need to stop them!"

Evelyn moved toward the door, preparing to confront them, but Dora grabbed her arm, holding her back. "Wait. We need a plan."

"Victor!" Evelyn shouted, stepping into the light. "We know what you're planning!"

Victor looked up, a smirk spreading across his face. "Ah, look who it is. The valiant heroes have arrived just in time to witness the grand finale."

The young man shrank back, eyes wide with fear. "We need to stop him," he murmured.

"Victor, this isn't what you want," Evelyn pressed, her voice steady. "You'll only hurt innocent people."

"Oh, but that's exactly what I want," Victor replied, his expression darkening. "They've pushed me out for too long. It's time they see the consequences of their actions."

Dora felt a surge of anger. "You're a coward, Victor. Hiding behind a fireworks display to make a statement doesn't make you powerful. It makes you dangerous."

He laughed, the sound sending chills down her spine. "And you think you can stop me? You're just a couple of girls playing at heroism."

"Just wait until I pull this lever," he continued, gesturing to the control panel, "and unleash a spectacle they won't forget."

Dora glanced at the panel, recognizing the array of buttons and levers that could set off the fireworks. "Don't do it, Victor! You don't have to go down this path."

The accomplice stepped forward, brandishing a knife that glinted ominously in the low light. "Back off, or I'll make sure you regret it."

Dora felt a surge of fear, but she forced herself to stay focused. "You don't want to hurt anyone," she said, trying to appeal to their sense of reason. "This isn't the way to solve your problems."

Victor's expression shifted slightly, uncertainty flickering across his features. "You don't understand. They need to pay."

"What if we could help you?" Evelyn offered, her voice calm and measured. "Let us help you find a better way to get what you want."

Victor hesitated, his grip on the lever loosening just slightly. "Help me? How?"

"By exposing the corruption and fighting back in a way that actually matters," Dora replied, seizing the opportunity. "We can work together to change things for the better, but this—this is just madness."

"You think I'd trust you?" he scoffed, but the hesitation lingered in his voice.

"Victor, you don't have to do this," the young man pleaded, stepping forward. "You can still walk away."

For a heartbeat, it seemed as though Victor might relent. But then the darkness returned to his eyes. "No, you're all wrong. This is the only way." He turned back to the control panel, his fingers hovering over the buttons.

Dora felt the weight of the moment pressing down on her. "If you press that button, you'll ruin everything, and you'll have to live with that forever."

Suddenly, the sound of footsteps echoed outside, and the tension in the room escalated. "Victor!" a voice shouted from the direction of the entrance. It was Oliver, accompanied by a group of vendors who had rallied together, ready to confront the threat.

Victor's eyes widened in panic. "We need to move! They can't find us here!"

"Now or never!" Evelyn exclaimed, taking a step forward. "This is your chance to turn back!"

In that moment, Dora lunged forward, determined to reach the control panel before Victor could activate the fireworks. She grabbed his wrist, and they struggled, the chaos intensifying around them.

"Stop!" Victor shouted, fighting against her grip. "You'll ruin everything!"

Dora could feel the power of the moment surging through her. "No, Victor! You're the one who's ruining everything!"

As the footsteps drew closer, the accomplice lunged at Dora, aiming to push her away. But Evelyn was faster, grabbing the accomplice's arm and wrestling them to the ground.

"Let go of the control!" Evelyn shouted as she struggled to maintain her grip.

Dora focused on Victor, feeling adrenaline coursing through her. With one swift motion, she managed to push him away, stumbling back into the wall as she reached for the lever.

"No!" he shouted, but it was too late.

Dora yanked the lever back, and a warning alarm blared through the control room, red lights flashing in rapid succession. The system had been disabled, and the fireworks display was halted.

"Now!" Oliver shouted, bursting into the room with a group of vendors who had come to assist.

"Victor! It's over!" one of the vendors called out, holding a cell phone ready to record.

In that moment, Victor realized the extent of his defeat. His face twisted in anger, but the panic in his eyes told a different story.

"Let's get out of here!" the accomplice yelled, scrambling to escape.

Dora turned to Evelyn, relief washing over her. "We did it! We stopped him!"

The group rushed forward, surrounding Victor and his accomplice as they attempted to flee.

"Don't let them get away!" Oliver shouted, his voice echoing through the room. "We need to hold them until the authorities arrive!"

Dora stood back, catching her breath, the reality of what had just happened sinking in. They had managed to avert disaster, but the fight wasn't over yet.

As they contained Victor and his accomplice, Dora knew that there would be more to face. But for now, they had saved the festival and protected their community from chaos.

"Let's get them out of here," Evelyn said, her voice steady. "We'll make sure everyone knows the truth about Victor and what he tried to do."

Dora nodded, determination igniting within her. They had taken a stand, and this was just the beginning.

Chapter 18: The Aftermath

The aftermath of the failed fireworks display rippled through the festival grounds like a shockwave. As the authorities arrived, a mix of fear and confusion hung in the air, casting a shadow over what had once been a jubilant celebration.

Dora stood with Evelyn and the young man, still catching her breath, as they watched the police take control of the situation. Victor and his accomplice were handcuffed and led away, their faces a mixture of anger and disbelief.

"Is this really happening?" the young man murmured, shaking his head in disbelief. "I thought he was invincible."

Dora placed a reassuring hand on his shoulder. "No one is invincible. Not anymore."

Evelyn nodded, her expression resolute. "We faced him together, and we won. That's what matters."

As they watched the crowd begin to disperse, whispers of what had occurred spread like wildfire. Some festival-goers looked shaken, others angry, while many were simply relieved that the situation had been contained before it spiraled out of control.

Oliver approached them, a concerned look on his face. "Are you all okay? I was so worried when we heard the alarm go off."

"We're fine," Dora assured him, though the weight of the day hung heavily in her chest. "But I'm worried about the aftermath. This isn't just going to blow over."

"Yeah, we need to address the community," Oliver said, glancing at the growing crowd that was still gathering near the control room. "They deserve to know what happened, and we need to reassure them."

Dora glanced around at the festival grounds, which were now littered with debris from the earlier festivities. Bright decorations that had once sparkled with life now felt like remnants of a different world. "Let's do it together. We can't let fear take hold."

As they moved to the center of the fairground, a few festival-goers began to gather around them, their faces painted with concern and curiosity. Dora took a deep breath, stepping forward to address the crowd.

"Everyone, please listen," she began, her voice steady but firm. "We know today has been chaotic, and many of you are confused and scared. But I want to assure you that we have stopped a serious threat to our community."

Murmurs rippled through the crowd as they processed her words. Evelyn stood beside Dora, her presence strong and supportive. "Victor was planning to harm this festival, to make a statement that would have hurt many innocent people," she added. "But together, we confronted him and ensured that no one was injured."

Dora glanced at the crowd, seeing the faces of her friends, neighbors, and those she had only seen at the festival each year. "We all deserve to feel safe during our celebrations. This community has always stood together, and we will continue to do so. Let's rebuild what was lost and show that fear will not win."

A cheer erupted from a small group near the front, and Dora felt a surge of hope. It spread like wildfire, igniting the crowd as they began to voice their support.

"That's right! We'll rebuild!" one woman shouted, her voice rising above the rest.

"We're stronger together!" another chimed in.

As the energy shifted, Dora could feel the weight lifting off her shoulders. She looked to Oliver, who nodded with a proud smile. Together, they were creating a new narrative—a story of resilience and strength, rather than fear.

Over the next hour, they discussed plans for restoring the festival, brainstorming ways to uplift the community spirit that had been momentarily shaken. They decided to turn the disruption into a rallying point, creating a series of events that would celebrate their unity and commitment to safety.

As the sun began to set, casting a warm glow over the fairground, Dora felt a renewed sense of purpose. They would not only salvage the festival but strengthen their community bonds.

"We'll organize a benefit concert," Oliver suggested, enthusiasm lighting up his face. "Invite local musicians, food vendors, everyone who wants to participate. Let's make it a celebration of our community!"

Dora smiled, the vision of a vibrant event sparking excitement within her. "That's perfect! We can showcase local talents and create a sense of normalcy. This is our chance to show that we will not be silenced or scared away."

As they made their way through the festival grounds, Dora felt a sense of determination rise within her. They would face any challenges together, united in their strength and resilience.

In the following days, the community came together to organize the benefit concert. Local businesses offered to donate supplies, musicians volunteered their time, and residents spread the word through social media, inviting everyone to join in the celebration of their community's strength.

On the night of the concert, the fairground came alive with laughter, music, and the scent of delicious food wafting through the air. Families gathered, children danced, and the atmosphere brimmed with joy.

Dora stood at the center of it all, feeling a deep sense of fulfillment. She watched as Evelyn mingled with festival-goers, laughter spilling from her lips as she shared stories of their encounter with Victor. The young man, whose name she had finally learned was Alex, helped set up the stage, his confidence blossoming in the supportive environment.

As the first band took the stage, Dora felt the weight of the past few weeks lift off her shoulders. They had triumphed over Victor's chaos, and now they were celebrating their strength together.

"Thank you for standing with us," Dora said to the crowd as the first notes rang out. "Let's show Victor that he cannot break us! We are stronger together!"

Cheers erupted, and the music swelled, enveloping the fairground in an atmosphere of hope and resilience. For every note played, Dora felt her heart soar, knowing they had overcome a darkness that had threatened their community.

As the night wore on, she found herself dancing among friends, laughter ringing in the air, a sense of belonging wrapping around her like a warm embrace. They had turned a moment of fear into a celebration of life, and for the first time in a long while, she felt truly free.

Chapter 19: Building New Foundations

As the final notes of the concert echoed through the fairground, the atmosphere buzzed with excitement and camaraderie. Dora felt a renewed sense of hope as she watched families laughing together, friends celebrating, and neighbors reconnecting. The benefit concert had been a resounding success, uniting the community in the face of adversity.

"Tonight was incredible," Evelyn said, wiping a tear of joy from her cheek as she joined Dora near the makeshift stage. "I can't believe how many people showed up!"

"I know! It's amazing to see everyone come together like this," Dora replied, her heart swelling with pride. "It's a reminder of what we can accomplish when we stand united."

"Definitely," Evelyn agreed, a grin spreading across her face. "But I think we can do even more. This could be the beginning of something bigger."

Dora's interest piqued. "What do you mean?"

"What if we created a community initiative— something ongoing that focuses on safety, support, and empowerment?" Evelyn suggested, her eyes lighting up with inspiration. "We could bring people together regularly, organize events that foster connection and encourage collaboration."

Dora considered the idea. "That's brilliant! We could host monthly gatherings to discuss community issues, offer workshops, and provide resources for people to get involved."

Evelyn nodded eagerly. "Exactly! We could include everything from self-defense classes to discussions on mental health, and even sessions on civic engagement. There's so much we could do."

As they discussed the potential initiatives, they were soon joined by Oliver and Alex, who were equally enthusiastic about the idea.

"This sounds amazing," Oliver said, his voice filled with excitement. "We can partner with local businesses to sponsor events, and I know a few folks who might be willing to help with the organization."

"Count me in," Alex added, his eyes brightening. "I've been looking for ways to contribute to the community since I moved here. This sounds like the perfect opportunity."

Dora felt a surge of gratitude for the support around her. "I love this. We can use the success of the concert as a springboard to get people involved. Maybe we can even start a social media campaign to keep the momentum going."

As they brainstormed, they began sketching out plans for their first community meeting. They settled on a date, booked a local venue, and designed flyers to spread the word. The excitement in the air was palpable, and Dora felt invigorated by the possibilities that lay ahead.

Over the next few weeks, they worked tirelessly to prepare for the inaugural meeting of their community initiative, which they decided to call **"Stronger Together."** The response was overwhelming—people from all walks of life signed up to attend, eager to be part of something bigger.

On the night of the meeting, the venue buzzed with anticipation. Dora stood at the front, her heart racing as she prepared to address the crowd. The room was filled with familiar faces and new ones alike, all ready to join the movement they had sparked.

"Welcome, everyone!" Dora began, her voice steady despite the nerves fluttering in her stomach. "Thank you all for being here tonight. This is a momentous occasion for our community, and I'm so grateful to see so many of you come together."

She glanced around the room, meeting the eyes of her friends and neighbors. "After everything that happened with Victor, we realized that our community is stronger when we work together. That's why we're here tonight—to create a safe space for open dialogue, support, and empowerment."

As she spoke, the room filled with murmurs of agreement, and Dora felt her confidence grow. "We've all experienced challenges, but by uniting, we can find solutions and lift each other up. Together, we can address issues that matter to us and create initiatives that strengthen our bonds."

The audience clapped and cheered, fueling her determination. "We'll be organizing workshops, discussions, and community events. We want your ideas, your passions—together, we'll shape the future of our community."

Evelyn stepped forward, sharing her vision for the initiative, while Oliver discussed potential partnerships and local resources. The enthusiasm in the room was contagious, and soon, attendees were sharing their own ideas and stories, igniting a sense of collaboration that filled Dora's heart with hope.

As the evening progressed, they broke into smaller groups to discuss specific topics. Dora found herself in a circle of neighbors sharing ideas on how to promote safety and awareness in their community.

"I think we need to focus on youth engagement," one woman suggested. "If we involve our kids and teens, we can instill the values of community service and responsibility in the next generation."

"Absolutely," Dora agreed. "We could start a youth council, empowering them to take part in decision-making and planning events."

By the end of the evening, the energy in the room was electric, filled with promise and possibility. They exchanged contact information and formed committees to organize various aspects of the initiative. Dora felt a sense of belonging that she had never experienced before—a realization that they were all part of something greater than themselves.

As the meeting concluded, and the attendees began to leave, Dora stood with Evelyn and Oliver, filled with a sense of accomplishment.

"I can't believe how well it went," Evelyn said, her cheeks flushed with excitement. "This is just the beginning, Dora!"

Oliver nodded, grinning from ear to ear. "We've got something special here. People are hungry for connection, and we've given them a reason to come together."

Dora looked around the venue, now emptying out but still echoing with the voices of their shared dreams. "I never would have thought that the events with Victor would lead to something so positive," she reflected. "It's incredible how the darkest moments can spark the brightest ideas."

In the days that followed, the initiative gained momentum, and "Stronger Together" quickly became a staple in their community. They hosted a series of events—workshops on mental health, self-defense classes, and even community art projects that brought people together to express their creativity.

Dora felt invigorated by the response and the connections being forged. Each event was a testament to the resilience of their community and the power of unity. She watched as friendships blossomed and people began to engage in conversations that had previously felt too uncomfortable or taboo.

As the months passed, the initiative continued to grow, and Dora found herself stepping into a leadership role she never expected to take on. She was frequently invited to speak at local events, sharing their mission and encouraging others to create similar initiatives in their own neighborhoods.

One evening, as Dora and Evelyn were wrapping up a community workshop, Evelyn turned to her, a smile lighting up her face. "Can you believe how far we've come since that day in the control room? It feels like a lifetime ago."

"It really does," Dora replied, her heart swelling with gratitude. "And to think it all started with a chaotic festival and a villainous plan. I never imagined we'd be here, but I wouldn't trade this journey for anything."

Their laughter filled the room, a sound of hope and joy. They had transformed their pain into purpose, turning their community into a sanctuary of support and growth.

As the sun set that evening, casting a golden glow over the fairground, Dora looked around, feeling a profound sense of belonging. Together, they had faced darkness and emerged stronger, ready to embrace whatever challenges lay ahead.

Chapter 20: A Personal Journey

As the days turned into weeks, the "Stronger Together" initiative blossomed within the community. Dora found herself in a whirlwind of activity, attending meetings, organizing events, and fostering connections among residents. Yet, amidst the excitement and joy of community engagement, she felt a nagging pull within her— a desire to delve deeper into her past, to understand the roots of her drive and commitment.

One evening, after a long day of planning the next workshop, Dora sat in her cozy living room, the faint light of the setting sun filtering through the curtains. She looked around at the familiar surroundings—the well-loved books on the shelves, the photographs of cherished memories pinned to the walls, and the comfortable couch that had been her refuge during many contemplative nights. It was in this space that she often found solace, but tonight, it felt different. The urge to confront her past gnawed at her.

Dora picked up a framed photograph of her family, taken during a summer vacation years ago. She was standing in the middle, her younger self beaming brightly, flanked by her parents and younger brother. They looked so happy, so carefree. But as she gazed at the picture, the memories that flooded back were bittersweet.

The laughter and joy in the photograph stood in stark contrast to the darker moments of her childhood—times when her family had struggled with the weight of their own challenges. Her parents had always worked hard to provide for her and her brother, but the stress often led to tensions that hung heavy in their home. Dora remembered nights spent in her room, listening to hushed arguments that echoed through the walls, uncertainty gnawing at her stomach.

It was during those moments that she had learned to be strong, to be resilient. She became adept at burying her emotions, putting on a brave face to shield her brother from the cracks that threatened their family's facade. Those experiences had shaped her, instilling in her a deep desire to help others find their strength in times of struggle.

Dora set the photograph down, a lump forming in her throat. She realized that her commitment to "Stronger Together" was not just about building a community; it was about creating a safe space for others who felt lost or alone. She wanted to ensure that no one else had to endure the same feelings of helplessness she had felt during her childhood.

With renewed determination, Dora reached for her journal, a place where she poured out her thoughts and reflections. She began writing about her past, weaving together the memories of her childhood, the struggles her family faced, and the lessons she had learned along the way. As she wrote, she began to see how her experiences had fueled her passion for community and connection.

The next day, as she prepared for the monthly community gathering, Dora felt a new sense of clarity. She decided to share her journey with the group, believing that vulnerability could strengthen their bonds even further.

When the meeting began, the atmosphere was warm and welcoming, filled with laughter and camaraderie. Residents of all ages gathered, eager to contribute to the discussions and share ideas for future initiatives. After a few updates and planning sessions, Dora stood up, heart racing as she prepared to speak.

"Thank you all for being here tonight," she began, her voice steady but tinged with emotion. "I want to take a moment to share something personal with you all—something that has shaped my journey and my commitment to our community."

The room fell silent, attention focused on her as she continued. "Growing up, my family faced many challenges. There were times when the weight of our struggles felt unbearable, and I often felt like I had to be the strong one, to hold everything together. But through those experiences, I learned the importance of connection and support."

Dora paused, glancing around the room at the faces of her neighbors—each one a part of her newfound family. "It's because of those moments of hardship that I believe in the power of community. I want to create a space where no one feels alone, where we can lift each other up in times of need."

As she spoke, she saw understanding and empathy reflected in their eyes. Many in the room had faced their own struggles, and the shared vulnerability created a powerful bond.

"I want you to know that it's okay to lean on each other," Dora continued, her voice gaining strength. "We're not just building a community; we're building a family. And together, we can face any challenge that comes our way."

A ripple of applause spread through the gathering, and Dora felt a swell of gratitude wash over her. In sharing her story, she had not only opened up but had also created a safe space for others to share their own experiences.

After the meeting, several attendees approached her, sharing their own stories of struggle and resilience. Dora listened intently, offering support and encouragement, feeling the connections deepening as they bonded over their shared experiences.

As the weeks turned into months, Dora noticed a shift in the community. More people began to open up during the gatherings, sharing not only their triumphs but also their vulnerabilities. It became a safe haven—a space where individuals could express their fears and dreams without judgment.

One evening, as she sat in her living room reflecting on the progress of "Stronger Together," Dora received a text from Evelyn.

Evelyn: *Hey! Do you want to grab coffee tomorrow? I have an idea I'd love to discuss!*

Dora smiled, excitement bubbling within her. She replied quickly, agreeing to meet and curious about what Evelyn had in mind.

The next day, they met at their favorite café, the smell of freshly brewed coffee wafting through the air. As they settled into a cozy corner booth, Evelyn wasted no time diving into her idea.

"I've been thinking," Evelyn began, her eyes sparkling with enthusiasm. "What if we organized a storytelling event? We could invite people from our community to share their stories—whether it's about overcoming obstacles, celebrating successes, or simply sharing their unique experiences. It could be a powerful way to foster connection!"

Dora's heart raced at the thought. "That's incredible! A storytelling event could provide a platform for people to express themselves and feel heard. It would strengthen our mission even further!"

They spent the afternoon brainstorming ideas, discussing how to structure the event, potential venues, and ways to encourage participation. As they planned, Dora felt a surge of excitement. This could be another step toward creating an even more profound sense of community.

As the date of the storytelling event approached, the excitement in the community was palpable. Flyers adorned the local shops, and social media buzzed with anticipation.

On the night of the event, the venue overflowed with attendees, the atmosphere electric with anticipation. As Dora stood at the front of the room, she marveled at the faces of her neighbors, each one representing a unique story waiting to be told.

The event unfolded beautifully, with individuals stepping up to share their experiences—stories of heartbreak and healing, of joy and laughter, of resilience and hope. As each person spoke, Dora felt a deep sense of connection among the audience, the threads of their lives weaving together into a tapestry of shared humanity.

At the end of the evening, Dora stood up once more, her heart full. "Thank you all for being here and for sharing your stories tonight. This is what 'Stronger Together' is all about—finding strength in our shared experiences and lifting each other up. I hope you leave tonight feeling inspired and connected."

The room erupted in applause, and Dora felt a profound sense of gratitude. She had come full circle—through the trials of her past, she had forged a path to a brighter future, not just for herself but for her entire community.

As the attendees began to leave, many expressed their gratitude to Dora and Evelyn for creating such a safe space for sharing. Dora felt a warmth in her heart, knowing that they had turned their pain into purpose, forging connections that would last a lifetime.

In the following weeks, the storytelling event became a monthly tradition, a cornerstone of the "Stronger Together" initiative. With each gathering, the bonds among community members deepened, and Dora's heart swelled with pride as she witnessed the transformative power of vulnerability and connection.

Chapter 21: Building Legacies

The storytelling events had become a cherished tradition within the community, a space where individuals gathered to share their truths and experiences. Dora felt a sense of fulfillment each time, knowing that they were forging connections that would last a lifetime. However, as she sat in the audience one evening, listening to heartfelt stories, a new idea began to take shape in her mind.

"What if we documented these stories?" she mused, her mind racing with possibilities. "We could create a book—a collection of our community's experiences and journeys. It could serve as a legacy for future generations."

As the event wrapped up that night, Dora shared her idea with Evelyn, who was immediately on board. "That's brilliant! We could invite everyone to submit their stories, poems, or even artwork. It could be a beautiful tapestry of our community's voices."

Excited by the prospect, they brainstormed how to approach the project. They decided to host a special session during the next storytelling event to encourage submissions, allowing participants to share what they felt comfortable with in a more intimate setting.

"Let's call it *Voices of Our Community*," Dora suggested. "It's a fitting title that encapsulates our mission."

As the weeks passed, Dora and Evelyn worked tirelessly to spread the word. They created flyers, posted on social media, and announced the project during community meetings. The response was overwhelming. People were eager to contribute, sharing their stories in various formats—some through written accounts, others through art, and even a few in the form of poems.

On the night of the special submission session, the atmosphere in the venue was electric with anticipation. Attendees filled the room, their energy palpable. Dora stood at the front, her heart racing with excitement and a touch of nervousness.

"Welcome, everyone! Thank you for joining us tonight," she began, her voice steady. "As you know, we're here to launch our project, *Voices of Our Community*. This is a chance for all of us to share our stories and preserve them for future generations."

The crowd erupted in applause, and Dora felt a rush of gratitude wash over her. "Tonight, we'll have a few people share their submissions with us, and then we'll open the floor for anyone else who wants to share. Remember, this is a safe space—feel free to express yourself in whatever way feels right."

As the evening unfolded, individuals took turns sharing their contributions—stories that ranged from heartwarming to heartbreaking, each one a reflection of their unique experiences. Dora felt honored to witness such vulnerability, realizing that every voice added a vital thread to the fabric of their community.

After the storytelling session, Dora and Evelyn encouraged everyone to submit their written pieces, artwork, or recordings in the coming weeks. They set a deadline for submissions and announced plans for a special launch event once the book was compiled.

Over the next few months, Dora dedicated herself to the project, gathering submissions, editing written pieces, and organizing artwork. She was deeply moved by the stories that poured in; they captured the essence of their community—the struggles, the joys, and the resilience that bound them together.

Dora often found herself lost in the narratives, reflecting on the shared humanity that resonated through each page. With each story, she discovered new facets of her neighbors—stories she had never known but that deepened her connection to them.

As the submission deadline approached, Dora felt a surge of excitement and nervousness. She wanted the book to reflect the true spirit of their community, honoring the contributions of each individual while celebrating the collective journey they had embarked upon.

On the day of the launch event, the venue buzzed with energy. Community members arrived, eager to see the culmination of their shared stories. The walls were adorned with artwork submitted for the book, vibrant displays that captured the spirit of the narratives.

Dora stood at the front, flanked by Evelyn and Oliver, her heart racing with anticipation. "Thank you all for being here tonight," she began, her voice filled with emotion. "This project represents the heart of our community—every story, every voice, is a testament to our shared journey."

The audience erupted in applause, and Dora felt her heart swell with pride. "Tonight, we celebrate not just the book but the connections we've forged and the strength we've built together. Each of you has played a vital role in making this happen, and I'm incredibly grateful."

As the event continued, they shared readings from the book, highlighting various submissions that resonated with the crowd. Each story was met with cheers, laughter, and even tears, as the audience connected deeply with the experiences being shared.

After the readings, they unveiled the book, *Voices of Our Community*, and handed out copies to the attendees. The joy in the room was palpable as people flipped through the pages, discovering familiar faces and stories intertwined with their own.

"Let's take this moment to celebrate our community," Evelyn said, her eyes shining with excitement. "This book is just the beginning! We can use it to inspire others, spread our message beyond our town, and create even more connections."

Dora couldn't help but smile at the thought. They had created something beautiful, a legacy that would endure long after the event. As people mingled, discussing the stories and sharing their thoughts, Dora felt a sense of belonging and pride wash over her.

That night, as she returned home, Dora reflected on the journey that had brought them to this moment. From the chaos of the festival to the darkness of Victor's influence, they had risen from the ashes to create a community that thrived on connection and vulnerability.

The *Voices of Our Community* book would serve as a reminder of their resilience—a tangible legacy that would inspire future generations to find strength in their stories.

In the weeks that followed, the book gained attention beyond their town. Local media outlets covered the launch, and soon, stories from *Voices of Our Community* began to circulate on social media. The community's message resonated far and wide, inspiring others to create similar initiatives in their own neighborhoods.

Dora found herself flooded with messages of gratitude from people she had never met, thanking her for sharing the stories that had moved them. Each message fueled her passion further, reminding her of the power of storytelling and the importance of connection.

As the seasons changed, so too did the spirit of the community. With each new story shared, they continued to strengthen their bonds, uplifting one another and nurturing the relationships they had built.

And amidst it all, Dora felt a profound sense of purpose. She was not just a witness to the stories unfolding around her; she was a catalyst for change—a force that had brought their community together in ways she had never imagined.

Chapter 22: Recognition and Opportunity

The excitement surrounding *Voices of Our Community* continued to grow, spreading beyond their town and capturing the attention of local media and organizations. Dora's phone buzzed incessantly with messages of praise, and the buzz around the project soon caught the attention of a well-known nonprofit focused on community building and empowerment.

One afternoon, as Dora was sorting through her emails, she noticed one from an organization called *Unity in Action*. The subject line read: **Opportunity for Collaboration: Community Empowerment Conference**. Her heart raced as she opened the email, reading with bated breath.

"Dear Dora,
We were thrilled to learn about your recent project, *Voices of Our Community*. Your initiative aligns beautifully with our mission to uplift and empower local communities. We would like to invite you to speak at our upcoming Community Empowerment Conference, where we will showcase inspiring stories from around the

region. This is a fantastic opportunity to share your journey and the impact of your project with a wider audience."

Dora could hardly believe what she was reading. Speaking at a conference? It was an incredible opportunity to highlight their community's stories and showcase the power of connection and resilience. She quickly shared the news with Evelyn and Oliver, who were equally excited.

"Dora, this is amazing!" Evelyn exclaimed. "You have to go! You can inspire so many more people with your message."

Oliver nodded in agreement. "Think about the connections we could make. This could help spread our initiative even further!"

Dora felt a mix of excitement and anxiety swirl within her. Speaking in front of a larger audience was a daunting prospect, but she knew it was a chance to elevate their community's voice. "You're right," she said, taking a deep breath. "I want to do this."

In the following weeks, Dora dedicated herself to preparing for the conference. She spent hours crafting her speech, drawing from the stories and experiences she had gathered during their journey. She wanted to emphasize not just the success of *Voices of Our Community* but also the struggles and triumphs that had shaped their collective narrative.

As the date of the conference approached, Dora felt both nervous and exhilarated. She rehearsed her speech in front of Evelyn and Oliver, who offered constructive feedback and encouragement. With each practice session, her confidence grew, and she began to embrace the opportunity rather than fear it.

Finally, the day of the conference arrived. Dora stood backstage, her heart pounding as she watched the audience fill the auditorium. The room was buzzing with energy, filled with community leaders, activists, and individuals passionate about making a difference.

"Next up, we have Dora Gray from DesignHive, who will share the inspiring story behind *Voices of Our Community*," the host announced, and Dora felt a rush of adrenaline as she stepped into the spotlight.

As she walked to the front, the audience's warm applause filled her with a sense of belonging. She took a moment to gather her thoughts,

looking out at the diverse faces before her—
each one a reminder of the interconnectedness
that had fueled her journey.

"Thank you so much for that warm welcome,"
she began, her voice steady despite the
butterflies in her stomach. "I'm honored to be
here today to share the story of our community
and the transformative power of connection."

As she spoke, Dora wove together the threads of
her journey—her childhood experiences, the
struggles she had faced, and how they had led to
the creation of *Stronger Together* and *Voices of
Our Community*. She shared stories from the
book, emphasizing the vulnerability and strength
of the individuals who had contributed.

The audience listened intently, nodding and
leaning forward as she painted a vivid picture of
their community's resilience. Dora felt the
energy in the room shift as she spoke, a sense of
connection forming between her and the
audience.

"This project is not just about preserving
stories," she continued. "It's about creating a
legacy that empowers individuals to share their
truth, to find strength in vulnerability, and to

build a community where no one feels alone. Together, we can foster connections that uplift and inspire."

As she concluded her speech, the applause that erupted felt thunderous. Dora's heart soared as she basked in the collective energy of the room. She had shared not just her story but the stories of many—each one a testament to the power of community.

After her speech, attendees approached her, eager to learn more about *Voices of Our Community* and the *Stronger Together* initiative. Dora was thrilled to connect with like-minded individuals who shared her passion for community building.

A representative from *Unity in Action* approached her with an enthusiastic smile. "Dora, that was an incredible presentation! We'd love to explore ways to collaborate further. Your project aligns perfectly with our mission, and we see great potential for partnership."

Dora's heart raced at the prospect. "I'd love that! I believe together we can reach even more communities and create lasting change."

Over the following weeks, discussions of collaboration between Dora's initiative and *Unity in Action* took shape. They explored ideas for workshops, mentorship programs, and community outreach initiatives that could empower individuals in underserved areas.

As Dora navigated this new opportunity, she found herself reflecting on how far she had come. The shy girl who once felt overwhelmed by her family's struggles had transformed into a confident leader, inspiring others to embrace their stories and find strength in connection.

Back home, the community continued to thrive, inspired by the recognition and opportunities that were emerging. Dora and Evelyn organized additional storytelling events, encouraging residents to share their experiences, fueling the collective spirit of resilience.

One evening, after a particularly successful gathering, Dora and Evelyn sat together, sipping tea and reflecting on their journey.

"Can you believe how far we've come?" Evelyn said, her eyes shining with pride. "It's incredible to think about the impact we're making."

Dora nodded, a smile spreading across her face. "It really is. And to think it all started with a desire to create connections. I can't wait to see where this journey takes us next."

As they spoke, Dora felt a sense of purpose surging within her. Their community was blossoming, and she was determined to continue fostering the connections that had changed so many lives.

With each passing day, she embraced the challenges and opportunities that lay ahead, knowing that they were not just building a community but creating a legacy of resilience, hope, and shared humanity.

Chapter 23: Facing Doubts

As the days turned into weeks following the conference, Dora felt the weight of her newfound recognition settle upon her shoulders. The initial thrill of being invited to speak at *Unity in Action*'s Community Empowerment Conference had filled her with hope and excitement, but as the reality of her position began to sink in, so did a creeping sense of self-doubt.

Each time she opened her email, a wave of anxiety washed over her. Messages of encouragement and requests for collaboration flooded in, but rather than feeling empowered, she often felt overwhelmed. Who was she to be at the forefront of this movement? The imposter syndrome gnawed at her, whispering insidiously that she was merely a girl from a small town, lacking the qualifications or experience to lead such significant initiatives.

One evening, as she sat at her desk, she found herself staring blankly at her laptop screen. She had been meaning to draft a proposal for a new workshop series in collaboration with *Unity in Action*, but the words wouldn't come. Instead, a flood of memories overwhelmed her—moments from her past that echoed the narrative of unworthiness.

"You're just a kid," her father's voice resonated in her mind. "What do you know about life? You can't change anything." The words that had stung her for so long now reverberated in her head, magnifying her insecurities.

"Dora?" Evelyn's voice broke through her thoughts, pulling her back to the present. She entered the room, her brow furrowed with concern. "Are you okay? You've been quiet lately."

Dora forced a smile, but it felt hollow. "Yeah, I'm fine. Just busy, you know?"

Evelyn wasn't convinced. She moved closer, her expression softening. "It's okay to not be okay. I've seen you shine, but I can also see the weight you're carrying. You've taken on so much, and It's okay to admit it's hard."

Dora's heart raced as she felt the dam of her emotions threaten to break. "I just—" she hesitated, unsure if she should share her struggles. "I feel like I don't deserve this recognition. I'm not qualified to lead this initiative. What if I mess everything up?"

Evelyn sat down beside her, placing a reassuring hand on her shoulder. "Dora, think about where we started. You've faced so much and overcome countless obstacles. Your journey is what makes you an inspiring leader. You're not just a voice; you're the embodiment of resilience. Don't let doubt overshadow that."

Tears welled in Dora's eyes as she absorbed her friend's words. "But what if I fail? What if I can't deliver on the promises we've made?"

"Failure is part of the journey," Evelyn replied gently. "Remember, you're not alone in this. We're all in this together. If you stumble, we'll pick you up. We're a community, and that's what matters."

Dora took a deep breath, letting Evelyn's words wash over her. She thought of all the individuals who had shared their stories and the strength they had shown. *Voices of Our Community* was not just her project; it belonged to everyone, and their collective spirit fueled her determination.

"You're right," she finally said, her voice steadier. "I can't let fear hold me back. I owe it to everyone to try."

Evelyn smiled, relief flooding her features. "That's the spirit! Let's brainstorm together and tackle that proposal. We'll make it amazing, and you'll see how powerful your voice can be."

With renewed determination, Dora set aside her doubts. Together, they dove into the proposal, weaving their ideas for the workshop series into a cohesive plan. The hours flew by as they brainstormed and collaborated, and by the time they finished, Dora felt invigorated. The fear that had once paralyzed her began to dissipate, replaced by a sense of purpose.

As they finalized the proposal, a notification popped up on Dora's phone. It was a message from *Unity in Action*, confirming the details of an upcoming meeting to discuss the workshop series.

"See?" Evelyn said, nudging her playfully. "You're already on your way!"

Dora grinned, the excitement bubbling back to the surface. "Thanks, Evelyn. I don't know what I'd do without you."

"Just remember, we're all rooting for you. You've got this."

As the days turned into weeks, Dora stepped into her role with renewed energy. The collaboration with *Unity in Action* blossomed, and they began crafting the workshop series, focusing on empowering community members to share their stories and develop leadership skills.

The first workshop was met with enthusiasm, drawing a diverse crowd eager to engage and learn. Dora found herself standing in front of a room filled with eager faces, her earlier fears fading as she shared her passion for storytelling and connection.

"Storytelling has the power to change lives," she declared, her voice strong and clear. "Each of you has a story that deserves to be heard. Together, we can create a ripple effect that transforms not just our community but beyond."

The energy in the room was infectious. Participants shared their experiences, and the atmosphere buzzed with inspiration and encouragement. As Dora guided discussions, she felt a profound sense of belonging—a realization that she was exactly where she was meant to be.

Weeks passed, and the workshops continued to thrive. Dora's confidence blossomed as she witnessed the impact of their work. Community members began to take charge, sharing their own stories and stepping into leadership roles.

But just when things seemed to be falling into place, an unexpected setback shook her confidence once more. A local news outlet published an article critiquing the effectiveness of the workshops, questioning the authenticity of the initiative and suggesting that it was merely a façade.

Dora's heart sank as she read the piece, feeling the familiar grip of self-doubt tightening around her. Had they truly made a difference, or were they just deluding themselves?

That evening, she confided in Evelyn again, her voice trembling as she shared her fears. "What if they're right? What if we're not making a real impact? I don't want to let anyone down."

Evelyn listened intently, her expression serious. "Dora, every initiative faces criticism. It's part of the journey. Remember, you're not just building a program; you're cultivating a community. The connections you've created are real, and they matter."

"But what if people stop coming to the workshops?" Dora asked, her voice laced with anxiety. "What if they believe the article?"

Evelyn shook her head, her eyes fierce. "Don't underestimate the power of your community. They've seen the change you're fostering

firsthand. Keep focusing on what matters—
sharing stories, creating connections. Your
authenticity will shine through."

Dora took a deep breath, grounding herself in
Evelyn's encouragement. She knew the road
ahead would be challenging, but she also
understood that every setback was an
opportunity for growth. With renewed
determination, she resolved to address the
criticism head-on.

The next workshop became a space for open
dialogue. Dora invited participants to share their
thoughts about the article and the impact of the
initiative. As stories unfolded, it became clear
that the connections they had built were
genuine and meaningful.

"Each of you has shown me what community
really means," Dora said, her heart swelling with
pride. "We've all faced challenges, but it's our
shared experiences that bind us together. Let's
continue to support one another and rise above
the noise."

As the weeks passed, attendance at the
workshops began to rebound, bolstered by the
community's commitment to the initiative. The

connections they had forged proved to be unshakeable, and Dora realized that her doubts were merely a reflection of her journey—a journey that had brought them together and inspired countless stories to be told.

With every challenge they faced, Dora learned to embrace her role as a leader, understanding that vulnerability and authenticity were strengths, not weaknesses. She was not just a voice; she was a vessel for change, carrying the stories of her community forward with pride.

Chapter 24: Personal Connection

Dora arrived at the community center with a renewed sense of purpose, ready to facilitate another workshop. The atmosphere buzzed with anticipation as participants trickled in, eager to engage and share their stories. She had found her rhythm, each session becoming a vibrant tapestry woven from the diverse experiences of those present.

As the workshop commenced, Dora introduced the theme of the day: **Resilience Through Storytelling**. She encouraged participants to reflect on moments in their lives that had tested their strength and shaped who they were.

"Each of us has faced challenges that have pushed us to our limits," she said, her voice steady and warm. "Today, let's explore those moments together, drawing strength from one another's stories."

As she guided the discussions, she noticed a newcomer sitting in the back—a young woman with a contemplative expression and bright blue hair, nervously twirling a silver ring around her finger. Dora smiled warmly at her, encouraging her to share if she felt comfortable.

After a few participants shared their stories of overcoming adversity, the blue-haired woman raised her hand. "Um, I'm not sure how to start," she admitted, her voice wavering slightly.

Dora nodded, offering a reassuring smile. "Just speak from the heart. We're all here to listen."

The woman took a deep breath, her gaze shifting between the floor and the group. "Okay. My name is Lila. I guess I'll share something that happened a few years ago."

Lila began recounting her story, her words initially hesitant but growing more confident as she spoke. She shared how she had struggled with her mental health throughout high school, feeling isolated and misunderstood. "I remember one night, I was at my lowest point," she said, her eyes shimmering with unshed tears. "I felt like I was drowning, and I didn't know how to reach out for help."

Dora listened intently, her heart aching for Lila. The pain in her voice resonated deeply, bringing forth memories of her own struggles. She recalled her tumultuous childhood, the moments of feeling invisible, and the realization that vulnerability could be a powerful source of connection.

Lila continued, sharing how she had eventually found solace in art and writing, channeling her emotions into creative expression. "It was through my art that I learned to speak my truth," she said, her voice gaining strength. "I started sharing my work online, and people responded. I realized I wasn't alone."

As Lila spoke, Dora felt a profound connection forming between them—a shared understanding of the battles they had both faced. The honesty in Lila's words resonated deeply, igniting a spark within Dora that reminded her of the very reason she had embarked on this journey.

After Lila finished her story, the room fell silent for a moment, absorbing the weight of her experience. Then, a ripple of applause broke out, and Dora encouraged everyone to express their appreciation for Lila's bravery.

"Thank you for sharing, Lila," Dora said, her voice filled with warmth. "Your journey is a testament to the power of resilience and self-expression. It's incredible to see how you've transformed your pain into art."

Lila's cheeks flushed with gratitude as she looked around the room, taking in the support surrounding her. "Thank you, everyone. I was really scared to share, but this community has made me feel safe."

As the workshop continued, more participants opened up, sharing their own stories of resilience and connection. Dora facilitated the discussions, her heart swelling with pride as she witnessed the healing power of storytelling in action.

After the session, Lila approached Dora, a mixture of excitement and nervousness in her eyes. "Thank you for creating this space. I didn't think I could share my story, but you made it feel safe."

Dora smiled, touched by Lila's words. "You did the hard part by sharing. It takes a lot of courage to be vulnerable. I'm glad you found your voice here."

"I've been thinking about starting an art project that combines storytelling and visual art," Lila said, her enthusiasm bubbling over. "I want to create a series of pieces that reflect the stories we've shared. Would you be interested in collaborating?"

Dora's heart raced at the idea. "Absolutely! That sounds incredible. Let's brainstorm how we can bring it to life. It would be a wonderful way to highlight the power of storytelling through art."

As they began discussing their ideas, Dora felt a renewed sense of purpose ignite within her. Collaborating with Lila could be a beautiful extension of *Voices of Our Community*, merging their passions to create something meaningful.

The following weeks were filled with creativity as Dora and Lila worked together, brainstorming and gathering stories from workshop participants. They envisioned an exhibition that showcased the intertwining of art and narrative, where each piece would represent a unique story of resilience.

Dora shared the idea with Evelyn and Oliver, who were excited and supportive. "This project could bring even more people together," Oliver remarked, his eyes shining with enthusiasm. "It's an incredible way to visualize the stories we've been sharing."

As the exhibition took shape, the excitement in the community grew. Participants began to submit their stories and artwork, and the anticipation for the event became palpable.

One evening, while Dora was reviewing submissions, Lila texted her. **Hey! Do you have time to chat? I've been thinking about the exhibition and wanted to share an idea.**

Dora quickly responded, eager to hear Lila's thoughts. "Of course! When can we meet?"

They arranged to meet at a local café that had become a favorite spot for the community. As they sat down, Lila's eyes sparkled with enthusiasm.

"I was thinking we could incorporate a live storytelling component into the exhibition," Lila suggested, her voice animated. "Maybe we can have an open mic where participants can share their stories alongside the artwork."

Dora's heart raced at the idea. "That's brilliant! It would create an even deeper connection between the art and the stories behind them. We could invite everyone to share their experiences and really bring the exhibition to life."

They spent the evening brainstorming logistics, exchanging ideas and excitement, the café buzzing around them. Dora felt invigorated by Lila's energy, their collaboration bringing out the best in each other.

As the exhibition day approached, Dora found herself reflecting on how much she had grown since the inception of *Voices of Our Community*. The vulnerability she had once feared had transformed into a powerful tool, allowing her to forge connections and foster resilience not just within herself but within others as well.

On the day of the exhibition, the community center was alive with energy. Colorful artwork adorned the walls, each piece accompanied by a narrative that spoke to the heart of resilience. As attendees arrived, Dora felt a wave of excitement wash over her, eager to see how everything would unfold.

The open mic began, and participants stepped up to share their stories, each voice a thread in the intricate tapestry they had woven together. Lila shared her own journey, her art a vivid backdrop to her words.

Dora stood among the crowd, a sense of pride swelling in her chest. This was what it meant to be a part of a community—supporting one another, sharing triumphs and struggles, and celebrating the beauty of vulnerability.

As the night came to a close, Dora reflected on the journey that had led them to this moment. She had faced her doubts and fears, but through the connections she had nurtured, she had also found strength.

With Lila by her side, they had created a space where stories could be told, where individuals could feel seen and heard. And as the applause echoed around her, Dora realized that she was not just a facilitator of stories; she was a part of a larger narrative—one of resilience, connection, and hope.

Chapter 25: Personal Growth

As the dust settled from the successful exhibition, Dora felt a wave of contentment wash over her. The stories shared, the connections forged, and the artistry displayed had created an environment bursting with hope and resilience. Yet, amid the joy, she found herself yearning for something deeper—an exploration of her own narrative.

In the days following the exhibition, Dora reflected on the personal stories that had resonated with her throughout the event. She had witnessed the power of vulnerability and the strength found in sharing experiences. Inspired by Lila and the community, she realized it was time to delve into her own creative outlet: writing.

Writing had always been a solace for Dora, a way to express her emotions and unravel the tangled threads of her thoughts. She recalled the journals she had kept over the years, filled with fragmented thoughts and poetic musings. Now, it felt like the perfect moment to transform those reflections into something more cohesive—a story of her own.

Determined to embark on this journey, Dora set aside time each evening to write. She found a cozy nook in her apartment, surrounded by the faint glow of fairy lights, and opened her laptop. The blank page loomed before her, both daunting and inviting.

With a deep breath, she began typing. The words flowed effortlessly as she wrote about her childhood—the challenges she had faced, the moments of despair and doubt, and the eventual spark of hope that had ignited her passion for community engagement.

Her writing became a cathartic release, a way to confront her past and weave it into a narrative that was both raw and transformative. As she revisited her memories, she felt the weight of her experiences lift, replaced by a sense of empowerment. The act of putting pen to paper—of transforming her story into something tangible—was liberating.

Dora soon found herself caught in a rhythm, dedicating hours to her writing. Each evening, she would pour her heart into the pages, exploring the themes of resilience, identity, and the quest for belonging. She incorporated the stories of those she had met in the community, intertwining their experiences with her own to create a tapestry of shared humanity.

As the weeks passed, Dora's manuscript began to take shape. She envisioned it as a collection of interconnected stories, showcasing the strength found In vulnerability and the power of community.

One night, while editing a particularly poignant chapter, she received a text from Lila: **Hey! Are you free to meet up? I'd love to chat about our next steps!**

Dora smiled at the message, excited to catch up with her friend. They agreed to meet at their favorite café, where they had first brainstormed their collaboration for the exhibition.

When they settled in with their coffees, Lila leaned forward, her eyes sparkling with enthusiasm. "I've been thinking about how we can keep the momentum going after the exhibition. What do you think about starting a monthly storytelling night?"

Dora's heart raced at the idea. "That sounds incredible! It would give people a consistent platform to share their stories and connect."

"Exactly! We could invite local musicians or artists to join us as well, creating an even more vibrant atmosphere. I think it could really build a sense of community."

As they brainstormed ideas for the storytelling night, Dora felt a surge of inspiration. "You know, I've been writing lately. I want to weave my experiences into my storytelling, just like we've been doing with the workshops."

Lila's eyes widened in surprise and excitement. "That's amazing! I'd love to read what you've written. Your voice is so powerful; it needs to be shared."

Dora felt a blush creep to her cheeks. "Thanks! I'm a bit nervous about sharing it, though. It's so personal."

"Trust me, vulnerability is where the magic happens," Lila replied earnestly. "Your story could resonate with so many people. It might even inspire others to share their own experiences."

Dora took a deep breath, her apprehension mingling with excitement. "Okay, I'll think about it. Maybe I can read a piece at the storytelling night?"

"Yes! That would be perfect!" Lila exclaimed, her enthusiasm infectious. "We can encourage everyone to share something, whether it's a story, a poem, or even a song. It'll be a celebration of our community."

As they continued to plan, Dora felt a newfound sense of purpose. This storytelling night would not only allow her to share her voice but would also provide a platform for others to do the same. It felt like the next natural step in their journey—a continuation of what they had built together.

Over the next few weeks, Dora worked diligently on her manuscript while helping Lila prepare for the storytelling night. They promoted the event through social media, reaching out to the community and inviting everyone to join. The response was overwhelmingly positive, and anticipation grew as the date approached.

When the night finally arrived, the atmosphere in the community center was electric. Strings of lights illuminated the space, and chairs were arranged in a cozy circle, creating an inviting environment for sharing. The scent of fresh coffee and pastries wafted through the air as attendees mingled, their excitement palpable.

As the event kicked off, Dora felt a mixture of nerves and exhilaration. She took her place at the front, standing beside Lila, who beamed with pride.

"Welcome, everyone!" Dora began, her voice steady despite the flutter of nerves in her stomach. "Tonight is all about sharing our stories and celebrating the strength we find in vulnerability. We've all faced challenges, and each of us has a unique voice that deserves to be heard."

The crowd erupted into applause, and Dora felt her heart swell with gratitude. She had created this space for connection, and now it was time to embrace the vulnerability that came with it.

As the evening progressed, participants took turns sharing their stories. Lila shared a powerful piece about her journey through mental health, and the room listened with rapt attention. Each story was met with encouragement, creating an atmosphere of support and compassion.

Finally, it was Dora's turn. Her heart raced as she approached the microphone, clutching her notes tightly. She took a deep breath, allowing the warmth of the room to envelop her.

"I want to share a part of my journey with you all," she began, her voice steadying as she glanced around the room. "Growing up, I often felt like I didn't belong. I struggled with feelings of isolation, and it took me a long time to find my voice."

As she spoke, she wove in the memories of her childhood, the battles she had fought, and the moments that had shaped her. The words flowed from her heart, each sentence resonating with the experiences of those present.

"I realized that vulnerability is not a weakness; it's a strength," she continued, her passion igniting the room. "Through sharing our stories, we build connections that empower us to rise above our struggles."

When she finished, the room erupted into applause, and Dora felt tears prick at the corners of her eyes. The validation and support from the community enveloped her like a warm embrace.

The storytelling night was a resounding success, and as the attendees mingled afterward, Dora felt a sense of fulfillment wash over her. She had faced her fears, shared her truth, and connected with others in a profound way.

As Lila joined her, a broad smile on her face, Dora felt the weight of her insecurities lift. "You were amazing, Dora! Your story was so powerful!"

"Thank you! I felt so supported up there," Dora replied, her heart still racing with exhilaration. "I never imagined I could share something so personal."

"Now you know you can!" Lila exclaimed. "You have a gift for storytelling, and I can't wait to see where this journey takes you."

In that moment, surrounded by the energy of their community, Dora understood that her journey was just beginning. Writing her story had become more than just a personal exploration; it was a way to inspire others, to foster connection, and to remind herself and those around her that they were never truly alone.

Chapter 26: A Moment of Doubt

The weeks following the storytelling night were a whirlwind of creativity and connection for Dora. She poured herself into her writing, eagerly sharing excerpts with Lila and even receiving feedback from workshop participants. The community she had built felt more vibrant than ever, and Dora's heart swelled with pride and gratitude.

Yet, amid the excitement, a flicker of doubt began to creep in. As she sat in her favorite nook one evening, surrounded by pages filled with her thoughts and emotions, she couldn't shake the nagging feeling that perhaps her story wasn't worth telling after all.

The voices in her head echoed, whispering insecurities that she had fought hard to silence.

What if no one resonates with your experiences? What if they don't see the value in your story?

Dora clenched her jaw, trying to push the thoughts away. She had witnessed the power of storytelling, both in herself and in others. So why was she suddenly questioning her own journey?

Feeling overwhelmed, she set her laptop aside and leaned back in her chair, staring at the ceiling as if the answer might fall from the sky. She needed perspective, a reminder of why she had started this journey in the first place.

As if on cue, her phone buzzed, breaking the silence. It was a text from Lila: **Hey, do you want to grab coffee tomorrow? I'd love to catch up!**

Dora smiled at the message, grateful for the offer. Perhaps spending time with Lila would help shake off the doubts clouding her mind. They agreed to meet at the café where they had brainstormed their storytelling night, a place filled with memories of collaboration and creativity.

The next day, as they settled into their usual corner, Dora noticed the warmth in Lila's eyes.

"I've been thinking a lot about the storytelling night," Lila began. "It was so powerful to hear everyone share their experiences. It made me realize how essential it is to keep this going."

"I completely agree," Dora replied, grateful for Lila's enthusiasm. "It felt like such a safe space for everyone. But I have to admit, I've been struggling with my own writing lately. I keep doubting whether my story is worth telling."

Lila's expression shifted to one of understanding. "I get that. Sharing our stories can be incredibly vulnerable. But you have to remember that your voice matters. Your experiences can inspire others, even if it doesn't feel significant to you."

Dora sighed, her fingers tracing the rim of her coffee cup. "I know, but I can't help but think that maybe I'm not interesting enough. I've been sitting with my manuscript, and I just feel stuck. It's like I've lost the thread of my own story."

"Have you thought about taking a break from the manuscript?" Lila suggested gently. "Sometimes, stepping back can give us clarity.

You could explore something new—like poetry or short stories—to reignite that spark."

Dora considered Lila's suggestion. "That might help. I think I'm so focused on getting it right that I'm losing sight of why I started writing in the first place."

"Exactly! Writing is about exploration and expression. It doesn't have to be perfect; it just has to be true to you," Lila encouraged, her voice steady and sincere. "Why don't we set up a little writing retreat? Just the two of us? We can go to a park or somewhere quiet and spend the day writing whatever comes to mind."

Dora's heart lifted at the idea. "That sounds amazing! I think a change of scenery would really help me."

They spent the rest of their coffee date planning their writing retreat, mapping out a location and packing snacks for the day. The prospect of stepping away from her manuscript and exploring new forms of writing filled Dora with excitement.

On the day of the retreat, they arrived at a serene park just outside the city, where tall trees provided a natural canopy, filtering the sunlight into soft, golden hues. Dora felt her worries begin to dissipate as they settled on a blanket, the sounds of nature enveloping them.

"I love this place," Lila remarked, glancing around at the vibrant greenery. "It feels like we're in our own little world."

As they spread out their notebooks and pens, Dora took a deep breath, inhaling the fresh air. "Okay, what do you want to start with?"

"Let's do a free-write exercise to warm up," Lila suggested, a playful glint in her eye. "We can write for ten minutes without stopping. No editing, no second-guessing—just let the words flow."

Dora nodded, feeling her heart race with anticipation. She picked up her pen and began to write, allowing her thoughts to spill onto the page without hesitation. The exercise felt liberating, and she lost herself in the rhythm of her writing.

When the timer went off, they shared snippets of their writing, laughter and encouragement flowing easily between them. Lila's pieces were filled with vivid imagery and emotion, while

Dora's words explored memories of joy, pain, and the moments that had shaped her journey.

"See? You have so much to say," Lila said, her eyes shining with excitement. "This is just the warm-up! Imagine what you can create if you let yourself dive deeper."

Feeling a spark of motivation, Dora scribbled down ideas for new pieces—short stories inspired by her experiences, character sketches, and even fragments of poetry. The more they wrote, the more liberated she felt, as if the weight of her insecurities was lifting with each stroke of the pen.

As the sun dipped lower in the sky, painting the horizon with hues of orange and pink, Dora turned to Lila. "I think I needed this more than I realized. Thank you for pushing me to explore."

Lila smiled warmly. "You don't have to thank me. This journey is just as much yours as it is mine. We're in this together."

With newfound clarity and motivation, Dora returned home that evening, her heart lighter and her mind buzzing with ideas. She had rediscovered the joy of writing—not as a chore or a means to an end, but as a form of expression that connected her to herself and to others.

That night, she sat down at her laptop with renewed vigor. She began drafting a short story based on a memory of a summer spent with her grandmother, weaving in elements of joy and nostalgia. The words flowed effortlessly as she lost herself in the narrative, her doubts replaced by the thrill of creation.

As the night deepened, Dora felt a sense of peace wash over her. She understood that doubt was a part of the creative process; it didn't define her worth or the value of her story. She was learning to embrace her voice, to explore her experiences, and to celebrate the journey of storytelling.

Chapter 27: Unexpected Feedback

Dora was buzzing with excitement as she prepared for the next community gathering, eager to share the new short story she had written. It was her first attempt at writing outside of her manuscript, and the experience had invigorated her creativity. She felt ready to show her work, confident that it would resonate with others.

The evening of the gathering arrived, and the atmosphere was charged with anticipation. The community center was filled with familiar faces—friends, neighbors, and fellow storytellers, all eager to share their latest works and experiences. As Dora entered the room, she caught sight of Lila, who was busy setting up refreshments at a table.

"Hey! You ready to share your piece tonight?" Lila called, her smile infectious.

"I am! I can't wait to hear everyone's thoughts," Dora replied, her nerves tingling with excitement.

As the event began, participants took turns reading their stories, each one more heartfelt than the last. Dora listened intently, feeling the bond grow among the group as they shared their truths. It was a reminder of why they had come together: to support one another in their journeys.

Finally, it was Dora's turn. She stepped up to the front, her heart racing as she held her notes in trembling hands. Taking a deep breath, she began to read her story—an exploration of childhood memories, the complexities of love, and the warmth of family. She poured her heart into every word, feeling the audience's energy feed her confidence.

When she finished, the room erupted into applause. Dora felt a rush of relief and pride wash over her, grateful for the supportive community surrounding her.

"Wow, Dora! That was beautiful!" Lila exclaimed as she joined her at the front. "You have a real gift for capturing emotions."

"Thank you! I'm so glad you liked it," Dora replied, her heart swelling with gratitude.

As the evening progressed, the attendees offered their feedback, praising Dora for her evocative writing. However, amidst the compliments, one voice stood out—Sarah, a fellow writer known for her sharp critiques and deep insights.

"Dora, I really loved the emotional depth of your story," Sarah began, her tone thoughtful. "But I think there are places where you could dig even deeper. Some of the details felt a bit surface-level. I'd love to see you really explore those emotions and experiences more fully."

Dora felt her heart sink slightly at the critique, unsure of how to respond. While she appreciated Sarah's feedback, her initial excitement faltered as she processed the implications of her words.

"Thank you for your honesty, Sarah. I'll definitely consider that," Dora replied, trying to keep her voice steady.

As the evening continued, Dora found it difficult to shake off the sting of Sarah's critique. The other positive comments began to fade into the background as she replayed Sarah's words in her mind. **Was her story really not deep enough? Had she failed to convey her emotions authentically?**

After the gathering, Dora lingered for a moment, watching as people mingled and celebrated each other's successes. Lila approached her, a concerned expression on her face. "Hey, are you okay? I saw that you seemed a bit quiet after sharing."

Dora forced a smile, but the doubt lingered. "I don't know. I mean, I really appreciated everyone's feedback, but Sarah's comments stuck with me. What if I'm not expressing my emotions as well as I thought I was?"

Lila frowned, placing a comforting hand on Dora's shoulder. "Dora, feedback is part of the process. It can be tough to hear, but it doesn't diminish the value of your story. You poured your heart into it, and that's what matters."

"I know, but I can't help but feel like I fell short," Dora admitted, her voice barely above a whisper. "I want my writing to resonate with people, to touch them the way others' stories have touched me."

"Trust me, it's a journey. Even the best writers face critiques. The key is to use it as a tool for growth, not as a measure of your worth," Lila encouraged, her tone firm yet kind.

Dora nodded, but the doubt lingered. As she walked home that evening, the shadows of uncertainty loomed larger than before. She replayed Sarah's critique in her mind, feeling a mix of frustration and self-doubt.

The next day, Dora sat at her desk, staring at the blinking cursor on her laptop. She opened her manuscript, hoping to dive back into the familiar comfort of her writing, but the words felt elusive.

After several minutes of staring at the screen, she slammed her laptop shut, frustration boiling within her. The joy she had felt while writing had been overshadowed by doubt. **Maybe Sarah was right. Maybe she wasn't meant to share her story after all.**

Dora sighed, feeling disheartened. Just then, her phone buzzed with a message from Lila: **Hey, do you want to go for a walk? I think it could be nice to get some fresh air.**

Grateful for the distraction, Dora replied quickly, agreeing to meet at a nearby park. As she walked, the crisp air filled her lungs, and the gentle breeze brushed against her skin, providing a welcome reprieve from her swirling thoughts.

When she met Lila, they strolled along the winding paths, surrounded by vibrant autumn leaves that crunched beneath their feet. Dora shared her frustrations, recounting the feedback she had received and how it had left her feeling lost.

"I get it. It's hard not to take critiques personally," Lila acknowledged. "But think about it this way: every piece you write is a step in your journey. You're evolving as a writer, and that's what matters most."

"Do you really think so?" Dora asked, her heart lifting slightly at Lila's encouragement.

"Absolutely! You're exploring new themes and styles, and that's a beautiful thing. It takes time to find your voice," Lila replied. "Instead of seeing Sarah's comments as a setback, try viewing them as an opportunity to push yourself further."

Dora nodded, feeling the weight of doubt begin to lift. "Maybe I do need to explore those emotions more deeply. It could lead to some interesting discoveries in my writing."

"Exactly! And remember, it's okay to be vulnerable. That's where the most authentic stories come from," Lila said, her eyes sparkling with encouragement.

As they continued walking, Dora felt a flicker of hope reignite within her. She realized that doubt was simply a part of the creative process—a challenge she could overcome with perseverance and support.

When they returned home, Dora opened her laptop again, determined to confront her insecurities head-on. She started revising her story, taking Sarah's feedback to heart. Instead of shying away from her emotions, she dove deeper, allowing herself to be raw and honest on the page.

With each keystroke, she felt the layers of her narrative unfold, exploring the complexities of her experiences and the richness of her memories. As the words poured out, the doubts that had clouded her mind began to fade, replaced by a sense of clarity and purpose.

Dora realized that writing was not just about the final product; it was about the journey of self-discovery and growth that accompanied it. Embracing the feedback she had received, she committed to evolving as a writer while staying true to her voice.

Chapter 28: A Romantic Retreat

The idea of hosting a writing retreat began as a fleeting thought but quickly transformed into a shared vision between Dora and Lila. After their enlightening walk in the park, Dora felt invigorated to connect with others in a more intimate and creative environment. They settled on a charming cabin retreat nestled in the woods, away from the bustle of city life.

Over the next few days, they meticulously planned the event, outlining writing exercises, group discussions, and time for personal reflection. With each detail they refined, Dora felt a renewed sense of purpose and excitement.

As the retreat weekend approached, they prepared a cozy atmosphere, setting up the cabin with comfortable seating areas, notebooks, pens, and plenty of snacks. The beauty of the surrounding forest added to the allure, promising inspiration and tranquility.

The day of the retreat arrived, and the air was filled with the crisp scent of pine. As guests began to arrive, Dora's excitement bubbled over. She welcomed each participant, introducing them to the cabin's inviting atmosphere. Among the attendees was Ethan, a new face in their community writing group. He was tall, with tousled dark hair and an easy smile that instantly put Dora at ease.

"Hey, I'm Ethan. I've heard great things about this retreat," he said, extending a hand. His warm gaze lingered a moment longer than necessary, and Dora felt a flutter of attraction.

"Hi, I'm Dora! I hope you enjoy it," she replied, shaking his hand. A subtle spark ignited between them, leaving her feeling slightly breathless.

Once everyone settled in, Lila kicked off the retreat with a warm welcome. "We're so excited to have all of you here! This weekend is all about exploring your creativity and finding your unique voice. Let's make it fun and fulfilling!"

As they moved into the first writing exercise, Dora found herself paired with Ethan. They sat across from each other at a rustic wooden table, the sun streaming through the windows, casting a warm glow over their workspace.

"Ready to dive in?" Ethan asked, his enthusiasm infectious.

"Absolutely! I love these exercises," Dora replied, feeling a buzz of energy.

They spent the next thirty minutes engaging in a prompt that required them to write about a moment that changed their lives. Dora found herself sharing a deeply personal memory, the words flowing effortlessly as Ethan listened intently, nodding in understanding.

"I can really feel the emotion in your writing," Ethan said, his voice low and sincere. "You have a gift for making the reader feel connected to your experiences."

Dora's cheeks flushed at his compliment, her heart racing. "Thank you! I appreciate that. Your feedback means a lot."

As the retreat progressed, Dora and Ethan found themselves gravitating toward one another, their conversations flowing naturally between writing prompts and personal stories. They shared laughter over silly moments, supported each other's creative endeavors, and even engaged in light-hearted debates about their favorite books.

During a break, while sipping coffee on the cabin's porch, Dora couldn't help but admire the serene landscape before her. "I love this place. It feels like we're in our own little world," she said, taking in the beauty of the tall trees and the sound of birds chirping in the distance.

"Yeah, it's incredible. It's the perfect setting for creativity," Ethan replied, leaning back in his chair, his gaze fixed on her. "I'm really glad I came here. I feel like I'm getting to know my own voice again."

Dora met his eyes, a moment of connection sparking between them. "I feel the same way. This retreat has been a breath of fresh air."

As the sun dipped lower in the sky, painting the landscape with hues of orange and pink, they transitioned into the evening's activities—a cozy storytelling circle by the fireplace. Each participant took turns sharing their pieces, and when it was Dora's turn, she felt a mixture of excitement and nerves.

She read her revised story, pouring her heart into every word. When she finished, the group erupted into applause, and Ethan's smile was bright and encouraging. "That was amazing, Dora! You really captured the essence of your journey," he said, his eyes sparkling with admiration.

"Thank you, Ethan. That means a lot coming from you," she replied, her heart fluttering.

After the storytelling circle, the group moved to the porch, where the stars began to twinkle against the darkening sky. Lila initiated a discussion about writing processes, but Dora found herself distracted by Ethan's presence beside her. They exchanged smiles and playful banter, and the chemistry between them crackled with electricity.

"Do you believe in writer's block?" Ethan asked, leaning slightly closer, his curiosity evident.

"I think it exists, but it's just a phase. It's like a journey to rediscover your passion," Dora replied, feeling her pulse quicken as their shoulders brushed.

Ethan nodded, his gaze steady on her. "What do you do to overcome it?"

"I explore different forms of writing, like poetry or short stories. It helps me reconnect with my emotions," she explained, her heart racing. "What about you?"

"I usually take a break and try to step outside my comfort zone. But I find that sharing my work with others helps break down those barriers," he said, his voice warm and inviting.

As the night wore on, Dora felt the weight of the world slipping away. In Ethan's presence, she felt a sense of ease and understanding, as if they were two souls on a parallel journey. The connection between them deepened with every shared story, every laugh, and every lingering glance.

Later, as they prepared for bed, Dora found herself unable to shake the feeling that something significant was blossoming between them. She lay awake in her cozy cabin room, thoughts of Ethan swirling in her mind, the flicker of attraction igniting her imagination.

Could this weekend lead to something more?

Dora drifted into a peaceful sleep, her dreams filled with words and possibilities, her heart open to the magic of storytelling and connec

tion.

Chapter 29: An Evening of Connection

The next day dawned bright and clear, with the sun filtering through the trees, casting playful shadows across the cabin. Dora awoke with a sense of excitement bubbling within her. She felt invigorated, ready to embrace whatever the day would bring.

After a leisurely breakfast, the group gathered for a writing workshop. Today's focus was on vulnerability in storytelling—a theme that resonated deeply with Dora. She felt inspired to share more of her personal journey, which had unfolded beautifully over the past few days.

As they settled in, Lila encouraged everyone to explore their emotions, inviting them to write from the heart without holding back. Dora could feel Ethan's presence beside her, and the thought both thrilled and unnerved her.

With her pen moving fluidly across the page, she wrote about her childhood fears, her struggles with self-doubt, and the profound joy of discovering her passion for writing. As she poured her heart onto the page, she glanced at

Ethan, who seemed equally engrossed in his writing. Their eyes met briefly, and a spark ignited between them, a silent acknowledgment of their shared experience.

After the workshop, Lila suggested they take a break and enjoy the serene beauty of the forest surrounding them. They headed outside, the sun warming their skin as they ventured along a winding path lined with vibrant wildflowers. Laughter echoed through the trees, and Dora felt a lightness in her heart as she walked alongside Ethan.

"Do you think we'll come up with something magical today?" he asked, his eyes glinting with mischief.

"Absolutely! Magic is all around us," Dora replied, her smile widening. "Especially when you're surrounded by creative energy like this."

They found a quiet clearing, the sounds of nature enveloping them. As they settled on the grass, Dora turned to Ethan, curiosity shining in her eyes. "What's been the most meaningful moment for you during this retreat?"

Ethan took a moment to think, his brow furrowed in concentration. "Honestly? It's been getting to know everyone, especially you. There's something special about connecting with fellow writers who understand the journey."

Dora felt her heart flutter at his words. "I feel the same way. It's refreshing to be surrounded by people who share the same passion."

The atmosphere shifted as Ethan's expression grew serious. "You know, I've struggled with sharing my writing for a long time. I've always feared that people wouldn't connect with it or that they'd judge me."

Dora nodded, her heart aching for him. "I understand. I used to feel that way too. But I've learned that vulnerability is what makes stories resonate. It's what makes us human."

Ethan's gaze met hers, and the moment hung between them, charged with unspoken emotions. "That's exactly it. I've been inspired by your willingness to share your truth. It's given me the courage to be more open in my own writing."

Dora felt a warmth spread through her, the sincerity of his words wrapping around her heart. "Thank you, Ethan. That means a lot to me."

As they continued to talk, the sun dipped lower in the sky, casting a golden glow around them. Dora could feel the connection between them deepening, a thread of intimacy weaving their hearts together.

When they returned to the cabin, the group gathered for another storytelling circle. Dora's heart raced as she considered sharing a piece that delved into her vulnerabilities, her struggles, and her evolving feelings for Ethan.

As the circle progressed, she listened to her fellow writers pour their hearts out, sharing their fears and triumphs. When it was finally her turn, she stood, clutching her notes tightly.

Taking a deep breath, she began to read, her voice steady despite the butterflies in her stomach. She spoke of her journey as a writer, the doubts that had plagued her, and how this retreat had awakened something profound within her. But as she continued, she found herself shifting focus, revealing her growing feelings for someone who had become an integral part of her experience.

"This weekend has been transformative for me," she confessed, her gaze drifting toward Ethan.

"It's not just about writing; it's about connections, relationships, and embracing vulnerability. I've found that allowing myself to be open has led to unexpected feelings for someone here."

The room fell silent, all eyes on her, but she felt only warmth radiating from Ethan, his encouragement evident.

When she finished, the group erupted into applause, but all she could focus on was Ethan, his expression a mix of surprise and admiration.

"Dora, that was incredible," he said as she returned to her seat, his voice barely above a whisper. "You were so brave."

"Thank you," she replied, her heart racing. "I just wanted to be honest."

As the evening progressed, Lila suggested they gather around the fire pit outside, where the flickering flames cast a warm glow across their faces. They settled around the fire, roasting marshmallows and sharing stories, the atmosphere charged with laughter and camaraderie.

As they exchanged tales, Dora felt a sense of belonging she hadn't experienced in a long time. But her attention kept drifting back to Ethan, who sat close, his laughter infectious and his presence magnetic.

Eventually, the group began to wind down, the conversations shifting to softer tones as the night deepened. Lila announced it was time for a final round of storytelling, and Dora felt the weight of anticipation in the air.

When it was Ethan's turn, he stood up, a confident smile on his face. "I'd like to share something as well," he said, his eyes locking onto Dora's.

As he spoke, he shared a deeply personal story about his struggles with self-doubt and the transformative power of vulnerability in his writing. Each word felt like a thread connecting him to Dora, and she couldn't help but be captivated.

When he finished, the group erupted into applause, but Dora was lost in his gaze, feeling as if the world around them had faded away.

"Thank you for inspiring me to share that," Ethan said, his voice low and sincere as he returned to his seat. "You've shown me the power of honesty in storytelling."

Dora's heart raced at his words. The chemistry between them had intensified, creating an undeniable connection that seemed to vibrate in the air.

As the night wore on, the group began to disperse, leaving only Dora and Ethan sitting near the fire, the embers crackling softly.

"I can't believe how much I've learned this weekend," Dora said, breaking the comfortable silence that had settled between them. "And it's all because of the incredible people here."

Ethan turned to her, a serious expression on his face. "Dora, I know this weekend is coming to an end, but I really want to stay connected. You've inspired me in so many ways, and I don't want this to be the last time we see each other."

Her heart leapt at his words, and she felt a rush of emotions. "I'd like that too. I really enjoy spending time with you."

Ethan smiled, a mix of relief and happiness lighting up his features. "Good. Then let's make it happen."

The fire flickered between them, casting warm shadows on their faces as they leaned in closer, the air thick with unspoken feelings. Dora could sense the shift in the atmosphere, the anticipation building as Ethan's gaze dropped to her lips, and she felt her heart race.

"Dora..." he began, his voice low, "there's something I need to tell you."

"What is it?" she asked, her breath hitching.

Ethan hesitated for a moment, his eyes searching hers. "I've really enjoyed getting to know you. You've opened up a side of me I didn't know existed, and I think I might be falling for you."

Dora felt her heart swell, warmth flooding through her. "I've felt the same way," she admitted, her voice barely above a whisper. "This weekend has been amazing, and I didn't expect to connect with anyone like this."

Their eyes locked, and in that moment, the world around them faded away. The tension that had been building culminated in a gentle intimacy, and as if drawn by an invisible force, they moved closer together.

With a shared breath, their lips met, a soft and tentative kiss that quickly deepened. It was a kiss filled with promise, connection, and the thrill of vulnerability. Dora felt her worries slip away as she surrendered to the moment, enveloped in the warmth of Ethan's embrace.

As they pulled back, both breathless, Dora knew that this was just the beginning. Their paths had intertwined in a way that felt destined, and she was ready to embrace whatever lay ahead—together.

Chapter 30: New Beginnings

The next morning, the sun rose over the horizon, bathing the cabin in a golden light. Dora awoke with a smile, memories of the previous night flooding her mind. She felt lighter, invigorated by her connection with Ethan and the experiences they had shared.

After breakfast, the group gathered for a final reflection session. They shared their insights from the retreat, discussing what they had learned about vulnerability, creativity, and connection. When it was Dora's turn, she spoke about the power of storytelling to forge bonds and the unexpected magic that had unfolded for her this weekend.

"I came here looking for inspiration, but what I found was so much more," she said, glancing at Ethan, who smiled back at her, his eyes shining with encouragement. "I discovered the importance of vulnerability, not just in my writing, but in my life. And I met someone who has inspired me to embrace that fully."

The group erupted into applause, and Dora felt a rush of gratitude. She had grown so much during this retreat, and she knew that her journey was just beginning.

As the retreat came to a close, they all exchanged contact information, promising to stay in touch. Dora and Ethan lingered at the edge of the group, their fingers brushing occasionally, sending sparks of electricity through them.

"Are you ready for the next step?" Ethan asked, a teasing glint in his eye.

Dora chuckled, her heart fluttering. "What do you mean?"

"I mean, we could explore more of our city together. There are so many hidden gems I'd love to show you," he said, his tone playful yet sincere.

"I'd love that! I want to see more of your world," she replied, feeling exhilarated by the prospect of their budding romance.

As they drove back to the city together, the air was filled with light conversation and shared laughter. Dora felt a sense of comfort and excitement, as if they had known each other for years instead of just a weekend. The chemistry between them was undeniable, and every shared glance sparked a sense of anticipation for what lay ahead.

Over the following weeks, they explored the city together, discovering quaint coffee shops, bustling art galleries, and beautiful parks. Each outing deepened their connection, and they reveled in their shared love for storytelling and creativity.

One afternoon, they found themselves in a quiet corner of a local bookstore, surrounded by shelves filled with stories waiting to be told. As they browsed, Ethan pulled a book from the shelf and handed it to her. "You have to read this. It's one of my all-time favorites."

Dora smiled, her heart swelling at his thoughtfulness. "Thank you! I can't wait to dive into it."

"Let's read it together," he suggested, his voice low and inviting. "We can discuss it over coffee."

"Deal," she replied, feeling a warmth spread through her. The idea of sharing a literary experience with Ethan excited her, solidifying their bond even further.

As they settled into a cozy café with their new books, Dora felt a sense of peace wash over her. The aroma of freshly brewed coffee filled the air, and they spent the afternoon immersed in each other's company, discussing their thoughts on the story and life in general.

It was during one of these conversations that Dora realized just how far she had come. The retreat had been a catalyst for her personal growth, and her relationship with Ethan had become a beacon of hope and love in her life.

One evening, as they strolled hand in hand along the riverside, the city lights twinkling in the distance, Ethan turned to her with a serious expression. "Dora, I want you to know that I'm grateful for everything we've shared. You've brought so much joy and inspiration into my life."

Dora felt her heart race, the sincerity in his eyes leaving her breathless. "I feel the same way, Ethan. You've made me see the beauty in vulnerability and connection."

He took a step closer, his gaze unwavering. "I want to explore this connection we have. I want to see where it takes us."

Dora's heart soared, and she couldn't help but smile. "I'd love that."

With a sense of mutual understanding, they leaned in for another kiss, the warmth of the moment enveloping them.

As they parted, the night stretched before them, filled with possibilities. Dora knew that her journey was far from over. With Ethan by her side, she was ready to embrace every twist and turn that lay ahead, both in her writing and in her heart.

Epilogue

Months passed, and the seasons changed, but Dora and Ethan's connection only grew stronger. They became each other's support system, encouraging one another through their writing journeys while building a relationship filled with love, laughter, and creativity.

Dora published her first collection of essays, drawing inspiration from her experiences at the retreat and the moments shared with Ethan. As she stood at her book launch, surrounded by friends, family, and the community they had built together, she felt an overwhelming sense of gratitude.

Ethan stood at the front, beaming with pride, his presence a constant source of encouragement. Their relationship blossomed, intertwined with their passions for writing and storytelling.

As they embarked on their next adventure, Dora realized that she had found more than just a partner; she had found a kindred spirit, someone who challenged her, inspired her, and made her feel alive.

Hand in hand, they ventured into the future together, ready to embrace the beauty of life, love, and the magic of storytelling.

THE END

www.ingramcontent.com/pod-product-compliance
Lightning Source LLC
Chambersburg PA
CBHW051252250726
48656CB00004B/1250